Historical, Literary, and Erotic Aspects of Lesbianism

Historical, Literary, and Erotic Aspects of Lesbianism

Edited by

Monika Kehoe, PhD

Historical, Literary, and Erotic Aspects of Lesbianism was originally published in 1986 by The Haworth Press, Inc. It has also been published as *Journal of Homosexuality*, Volume 12, Numbers 3/4, May 1986.

Harrington Park Press
New York • London

ISBN 0-918393-21-3

Published by

Harrington Park Press, Inc.   EUROSPAN/Harrington
28 East 22 Street   3 Henrietta Street
New York, NY 10010-6194   London WC2E 8LU England

Harrington Park Press, Inc., is a subsidiary of The Haworth Press, Inc., 28 East 22 Street, New York, New York 10010-6194.

Historical, Literary, and Erotic Aspects of Lesbianism was originally published in 1986 by The Haworth Press, Inc. It has also been published as *Journal of Homosexuality,* Volume 12, Numbers 3/4, May 1986.

Cover design by Marshall Andrews.

Library of Congress Cataloging in Publication Data

Historical, literary, and erotic aspects of lesbianism.

   Reprint. Originally published under title:
Historical, literary, and erotic aspects of lesbianism. New York : Haworth Press, 1986.
   Also published as Journal of Homosexuality, v. 12, nos. 3/4, Spring/Summer 1986.
   Includes bibliographies and index.
   1. Lesbianism—United States. I. Kehoe, Monika.
HQ75.6.U5H57   1986b   306.7'663'0973   86-14310
ISBN 0-918393-21-3

CONTENTS

The *Journal of Homosexuality* is devoted to theoretical, empirical, and historical research on homosexuality, heterosexuality, sexual identity, social sex roles, and the sexual relationships of both men and women. It was created to serve the allied disciplinary and professional groups represented by psychology, sociology, history, anthropology, biology, medicine, the humanities, and law. Its purposes are:

  a) to bring together, within one contemporary scholarly journal, theoretical empirical, and historical research on human sexuality, particularly sexual identity;

  b) to serve as a forum for scholarly research of heuristic value for the understanding of human sexuality, based not only in the more traditional social or biological sciences, but also in literature, history and philosophy;

  c) to explore the political, social, and moral implications of research on human sexuality for professionals, clinicians, social scientists, and scholars in a wide variety of disciplines and settings.

EDITOR

JOHN P. DE CECCO, PhD, *Professor of Psychology and Human Sexuality and Director, Center for Research and Education in Sexuality (CERES), and Director, Human Sexuality Studies, San Francisco State University*

ABSTRACTS AND BOOK REVIEW EDITOR

ANA VILLAVICENCIO-STOLLER, *Center for Research and Education in Sexuality, San Francisco State University*

MANUSCRIPT EDITOR

NORMAN C. HOPPER, *Center for Research and Education in Sexuality, San Francisco State University*

FOUNDING EDITOR

CHARLES C. SILVERSTEIN, PhD, *New York City*

NORMA MCCOY, PhD, *Professor of Psychology, San Francisco State University*
WILLIAM F. OWEN, Jr., MD, *Founder, Bay Area Physicians for Human Rights, San Francisco*
JAY PAUL, PhD (cand.), *Clinical Psychology, University of California, Berkeley*
KENNETH PLUMMER, PhD, *Lecturer in Sociology, University of Essex, England*
DIANE RICHARDSON, MA, *Lecturer in Sociological Studies, University of Sheffield, England*
STEVEN J. RISCH, PhD, *Assistant Professor of Entomology, University of California, Berkeley*
MICHAEL ROSS, PhD, *Senior Demonstrator in Psychiatry, The Flinders University of South Australia, Bedford Park, South Australia*
RITCH SAVIN-WILLIAMS, PhD, *Associate Professor of Human Development and Family Studies, Cornell University*
GUNTHER SCHMIDT, PhD, *Professor, Abteilung fur Sexualforschung, Universitats-Krankenhaus, Universitat Hamburg*
FREDERICK SUPPE, PhD, *Professor, Committee on the History and Philosophy of Science, University of Maryland, College Park*
ROB TIELMAN, Dr. Phil., *Professor, Interfacultaire werkgroep homostudies, Riksuniversiteit Utrecht*
JEFFREY WEEKS, M. Phil., PhD, *Social Work Studies, University of Southampton, England*
JACK WIENER, MA, *Retired, National Institute of Mental Health, Rockville, Maryland*
WAYNE S. WOODEN, PhD, *Associate Professor of Behavioral Science, California State Polytechnic University, Pomona*

Foreword

Women's homosexual conduct and relationships have contrasted with those of men largely because female and male sexuality have been often conceived as distinct, complementary forms preordained by nature. Although this biological view may well describe the sexuality of female and male animals, its application to human sexuality is only justified if one views human sexuality as nature's invention for assuring the propagation of the race. The articles in these issues on lesbianism quite clearly show that women's sexuality has many facets, that it can be its own source of gratification quite apart from men, and that, like men's sexuality, it can be intricately woven into the fabric of their lives and relationships, particularly with other women.

Both in the present collection on lesbianism and the previous collection on anthropology, edited by Evelyn Blackwood, a refreshingly new view of women's sexuality emerges from the pages of the *Journal*.

I congratulate Dr. Kehoe, the guest editor of this collection, for its broad interdisciplinary sweep which embraces history, literature, and social science research. I greatly appreciate the perseverance she has shown over a period of three years in soliciting and editing the papers and cooperating with the *Journal* editorial staff. I deeply appreciate the contributions of the authors and their willingness to respond to the successive editing of their manuscripts. Finally I thank Norman Hopper, the *Journal*'s manuscript editor, for his devotion to duty and detail, and Mrs. Corlyn Cognatta, my editorial assistant, and Mrs. Ana Villavicencio-Stoller, my administrative assistant, for their capable and loyal help.

John P. De Cecco, PhD
Editor

1

Introduction

Monika Kehoe, PhD
San Francisco State University

The *Journal of Homosexuality* may have been criticized from time to time for its attention to lesbian concerns and the number of women contributors, but a review of the tables of contents of the *Journal,* from its founding in 1974, shows that at least one-fourth of the articles have been devoted to a consideration of the female experience, and that 73 women authors have contributed to its pages. Several women have served on its editorial board. This may not be quantitative equality of presentations, but considering the relatively few female scholars who have investigated lesbianism, it represents a meritorious attempt by the editor to include available manuscripts in the *Journal.*

Now at last we are able to present the first issues entirely concerned with women and homosexuality. We hope they are the predecessors of many articles to come, as research on lesbianism expands and proliferates.

Although all 12 articles on the following pages are about women, this issue presents a female guest editor, and female book reviewers as well. We are glad to have three male authors among the contributors. In our call for papers, we asked writers to focus on either lesbian history, literature, or sexuality. Due to the large number submitted, we regret not being able to publish all of the fine manuscripts we received on these subjects.

The historical theme prevails in the first four articles. In the first two, by Kendall and Faderman, we see what hap-

Dr. Kehoe, a retired university professor who has taught in Africa, Asia, Australia and Canada and who retired from the University of Guam in 1977, is a member of the board of consulting editors of the *Journal of Homosexuality,* and a member of the National Council on Aging and the American Society for Aging. Correspondence should be addressed to Dr. Kehoe, 87 Banks Street, San Francisco, CA 94110.

pened to the lesbian heroine in the course of her appearance on the English stage from the late 1600s to the mid-1800s, and the shift from social acceptance to rejection of love between women from the 1700s to the 1900s.

In "Strange Country This," Grahn introduces the reader to a fascinating chapter in American history, one unknown to most of us. She leads us through the gay tribal customs of the American Indians and reveals their attitudes toward homosexuality as very different from the homophobia prevalent after the white man's advent. Hall's review of the lesbian corporate experience is a window on the contemporary history of women in the workplace and focuses on the struggle of a particularly discredited group to make a space for themselves on the career ladder.

With the contributions of Russ and Adams in the next two papers, we have considerations of the lesbianism of one of the most intriguing figures in 20th century literature, Willa Cather. The seventh and eighth articles deal with the third topic, namely sexuality. Brown describes her experience as a therapist working with lesbian clients, while the co-authors of "Sexual Fulfillment of Heterosexual, Bisexual and Homosexual Women," Bressler and Lavender, survey and present their findings. Everard's account of homosexuality among women in the Netherlands in the last century, which raises class issues as a pattern for disparity, further embellishes lesbian history. Finally, a report on the first study devoted exclusively to lesbians over 65 concludes the article section.

Five book reviews and two brief papers, the first a "Note" by Cruikshank on May Sarton, a contemporary writer much admired by the lesbian community, and a "A Portrait of the Older Lesbian" by Kehoe, complete the issue.

Kathryn Kendall, the author of the first article, "From Lesbian Heroine to Devoted Wife: Or, What the Stage Would Allow," gives the reader some insight into the treatment of lesbianism on the English stage from the late 17th to the mid-19th century. She examines the playwright's sources and how they departed from them to satisfy the different audiences of their eras. The tightening up of the conjugal family and the patriarchal suppression of women, for example, are two of the trends she mentions, as well as the power of audiences to influence playwrights and suppress presentation in the theater of any significant relationships between women.

In her article, "Love Between Women in 1928: Why Progressivism is Not Always Progress," Lillian Faderman introduces the reader to the change in the perception of romantic attachments between women. These attachments which were socially acceptable in the 18th and 19th centuries came to be seen as morbid, abnormal, and pathetic in the early 20th century. Besides Hall's *The Well of Loneliness,* Faderman tells us that other books celebrating woman-for-woman love created the fictional lesbian as an eccentric and a queer. She goes on to explore the influences of World War I and Freud on popular thought, along with the general "masculinization" of the female, which, as she points out, threatened the social institutions based on heterosexuality and aroused antagonism toward sexually deviant women. The author takes us through the excesses of the sexual revolution, wherein she describes the effects of birth control and the introduction of the automobile as a setting for courtship and intimacy—effects that contributed to the pressures to engage in heterosexuality. With these increased pressures came the realization that women were sexual beings; in the process, love between women fell into the category of perversion.

In the preface to her book, *Another Mother Tongue,* Judy Grahn refers to a chapter of that book (reproduced herein) by saying "Chapter 3 establishes the high public positions frequently held by gay people in American Indian Tribes in the recent past." She also describes how white culture suppressed Indian gay tradition and how the spring of Indian cultural values in the Southwest was desiccated by the drought of Anglo-European condemnation.

The plight of working lesbians and the strategies they use to deal with hostile corporate environments are described by Marny Hall in her article, "The Lesbian Corporate Experience." Through taped interviews with lesbian employees of corporations, she was able to analyze and describe the complex way in which they managed discrediting information about themselves.

In the two papers on Willa Cather, written in response

to our request for manuscripts on literature, the "masquerade" of a famous literary figure is exposed by the searching eyes of two scholars, Joanna Russ and Timothy Dow Adams, who examine her work and her biographies for clues as to her true identity.

Laura Brown, a psychotherapist, covers "a much neglected aspect of therapy" with lesbian clients in her article, namely, the treatment of sexual dysfunction, the roots of which can be found in cultural homophobia and misogyny. The trend in treatment in the last few years, she writes, has been toward supporting lesbian clients in their alternative lifestyles, rather than trying to "cure" them as was previously the case in psychotherapy. Even so, some lesbians, suffering from "internalized oppression," manifest types of sexual dysfunction similar to those of heterosexual women. Consequently, for therapists to be effective with lesbian clients, they must be aware of and monitor their own internalized homophobia.

Lauren Bressler and Abraham Lavender stress in their article, "Sexual Fulfillment of Heterosexual, Bisexual, and Homosexual Women," the fallacy of a heterosexual-homosexual dichotomy in the study of female sexuality. They also indicate how recent the research on female sexual response and fulfillment is and how more knowledge needs to be accumulated from subsequent studies in this, until now, relatively neglected area of research.

Our international contributor, Myriam Everard of The Netherlands, presents an intriguing discussion of the question: Is the homosexual woman of the 20th century the medical transformation of the 19th century romantic friend?

And finally, a pioneer report on lesbians over 65 which investigates their present life situation, educational background, psycho/social concerns, economic and occupational status, and physical and mental health, concludes the articles section of this issue.

Two short papers, "A Note on May Sarton" by Margaret Cruikshank and a "A Portrait of the Older Lesbian" by the guest editor, are interposed before the Book Review section in which five literary contributions by current lesbian writers are re-examined.

We hope the readers of this special lesbian issue of the

Journal of Homosexuality will be as gratified to read the work of the scholars presented here as we are to publish it. Perhaps now university departments that have denied approval of lesbian research proposals solely because of their subject matter will be persuaded to allow, and even support, graduate students and faculty wishing to pursue this long-neglected field of inquiry.

From Lesbian Heroine
to Devoted Wife:
Or, What the Stage
Would Allow

Kathryn Kendall, PhD
University of Texas

ABSTRACT. Plays written by English women on the same historical subject appeared in 1696 and 1841. The earlier play, written in a period of active feminism, features Agnes de Castro as a
lesbian heroine, probably the first in English stage history. The
second, written in the age of Solomon Grundy, characterizes de
Castro as a self-sacrificing, devoted heterosexual wife. Since both
plays were written by women who would now be defined as lesbians, the treatment of the heroine seems more a reflection of
audience than author. Study of the two plays with their sources
and their authors' lives reveals much about audiences and the
pressures a homophobic society can exert on lesbian artists who
write for a living.

INTRODUCTION

Two English playwrights, Catharine Trotter (1679–1749)
and Mary Russell Mitford (1787–1855), wrote plays on the
same historical subject, a tragic 14th-century love triangle
involving two women and a man. Trotter's play, performed
in 1696, is about the love of two women and how that love
triumphs over the conflict caused by a man. Trotter's
Agnes de Castro is probably the first lesbian heroine in
English stage history. Mitford's play of 1841 is about two

Kathryn Kendall has a PhD in theater history from the University of Texas
at Austin. She holds BA and MA degrees in English from the University of
New Orleans and has worked as an actress and writer for almost 20 years. Her
work has been published in *Heresies, Off Our Backs, The Feminist Review,
Feminary,* and in Vol. 1 of Judy Grahn's anthology, *True to Life Adventure
Stories.* She is a member of the Feminist Writers Guild. Reprint requests may
be addressed to the author, Drama Department, University of Texas, Austin,
TX 78712.

9

women competing for the same man and the conflict, for
the man, between love and duty. Mitford's Inez de Castro
is a self-sacrificing, single-mindedly heterosexual wife.

A glance at the sources and at other playwrights' treatments of the same legend leaves no doubt that Trotter and
Mitford used their treatments of the story to express distinct moral, sexual, and social viewpoints. In order to understand what those viewpoints were, it is useful to examine the playwrights' sources, to consider briefly their
lives, and to assess the different audiences for which the
plays were written.

BACKGROUND

The story of Inez de Castro has fascinated playwrights
for centuries, and several studies describe how various authors treated the story.[1] According to these studies, the
legend was first dramatized during Spain's "Golden Age"
(*ca.* 1580–1680) in versions written by Lope de Vega,
Mexia de Lacerda, Jeronimo Bermudez, Antonio Ferreira,
and Velez de Guevara. Later, French and Italian plays
appeared by Houdar de La Motte (1723), Victor Hugo
(1818), D. Bertoletti (1826), Henri de Montherlant (1942),
and Charles Ducros (1949).

All the men's plays center on the male of the famous
threesome and the division of his loyalties between the
woman he was contracted to marry but for whom he feels
no attraction and her relative or servant, Inez, to whom he
is irresistibly drawn. In the men's plays, the prince sometimes marries one woman, sometimes the other; sometimes
he marries one and gets children by the other, or by both.
Some of the men's plays deal with the hero's relation to his
father, the King of Portugal, who ordered Inez put to
death; other plays dramatize the King's conflict between
concern for his son's happiness and concern for the good of
the country. So far as any one of the comparative studies
note, no European women playwrights treated the legend
of Inez, and predictably, none of the male playwrights focused on relations between the two women.

Relying on the Portugese chronicles of Pedro Lopez de

Ayala (ca. 1670), Suzanne Cornil summarizes the historical
background for the legend as follows. Constance married
Don Pedro by contract and brought Inez with her to Portugal; Don Pedro fell in love with Inez and produced offspring by both women. Constance died young and the
King, fearing his son would marry Inez and legitimize their
offspring, thus leading to squabbles over succession, ordered Inez decapitated.[2]

Ayala was probably Mitford's major source, for in a letter dated March 30, 1827, Mitford describes her plans for
the play in detail, explaining:

> There are two French plays, one English, and one
> Spanish, on the subject, but I follow none of them; my
> plot is my own, and closer to the narrative given in an
> old Portuguese chronicle.[3]

Presumably the English play to which Mitford refers is that
of Catharine Trotter, and the two French were those of La
Motte and Hugo. Mitford stayed faithful to Ayala, adding
her own emphasis and borrowing a bit from Trotter in the
last act.

Trotter's main source, without question, was the 1688
translation by Aphra Behn of a French novel by Jean Bap-
tiste Brilhac. Behn's translation, entitled *The History of
Agnes de Castro,* has been reprinted in two modern versions,
one edited by Montague Summers and the other by Ernest
Baker.[4] Trotter borrowed whole sections of Behn's work verbatim, but like Mitford, Trotter created her own emphasis
and characterization, particularly in the case of Agnes.

THE PLAYS

Trotter's *Agnes de Castro* (1915/1696)[5]

Elvira: . . . That Poison Jealousie
Destroys the strongest Bonds of Blood, or
    Friendship;
Constantia cannot think the Prince loves Agnes,
But she must hate, and treat her as a Rival.

Act I, scene 1, p. 1

Thus, in an opening scene reminiscent of the opening of
Othello, Elvira, Trotter's female villain, plots to undermine
the friendship between Constantia and Agnes, depending
on jealousy to do the job. But the whole action of the play
is to prove Elvira wrong. Constantia never hates or treats
Agnes as a rival, and the bonds of the friendship are never
broken. Suspense is maintained throughout; several times
it seems Constantia will turn against Agnes. But the play is
set up to prove, by the last act, that love between women
can conquer all.

The play begins with the following circumstances. Don
Pedro is married to Constantia. He secretly loves Agnes de
Castro, but she loves only Constantia. Constantia loves
Don Pedro and Agnes equally. There are two villains:
Elvira, Don Pedro's former mistress, who hopes to cause a
split between Constantia and Agnes so that Agnes will go
back to Spain; and Alvaro, brother of Elvira, who wants to
marry Agnes, by force if necessary.

The first scene between the two women takes place in
Constantia's room, as Agnes enters and they express their
mutual love:

> **Princess:** My Agnes! Art thou come! My Souls best
> Comfort, Thou dear Relief to my oppressing Cares:
> My griefs have lost already half their force,
> They vanish at thy sight, like Mists, before the Sun.
> **Agnes:** What Mists, what Clouds are these,
>   o'respread your soul?
> Which do like those that wou'd obscure the Sun,
> Whilst they but seem to darken the bright Mind,
> Cast a sad Gloom on all the World beneath (p.3).

Constantia's gloom comes from her awareness that Don
Pedro doesn't love her and her suspicion that he must be in
love with someone else. Agnes can't believe this and warns
Constantia not to be jealous. Constantia replies, "Leave it,
I would believe I have thy Heart,/The only comfort for the
loss of his;/For you are both so equal dear to me" (p. 5).

At this point Elvira's emissary enters with a love poem
stolen from Don Pedro (lifted verbatim from Behn's translation of the French novel) which names Agnes as his se-

cret love. Here Trotter exercises good dramatic sense in having Constantia and Agnes receive and read the poem together. (In the novel Constantia is alone when she finds the poem left by Elvira in her room.) Agnes, utterly shocked for she hasn't guessed Don Pedro's feelings, goes into hysterics, fearing Constantia will hate her; Constantia reprimands Agnes, "That thought was too injurious from a Friend" (p.7). Gradually Agnes calms down, and Constantia reassures her, "Thou dear, thou less my Rival, than my Friend." We have to imagine what the two actresses did onstage at that moment, for it was not customary to include stage directions in the published script. But just at that moment Don Pedro enters, sees the missing poem, and knows he has been discovered. Agnes quickly exits, leaving Don Pedro and Constantia to play out a bizarre husband-and-wife scene.

Consumed with guilt, Don Pedro begs Constantia, "Rail at me, Curse me, Hate me if thou canst" (p.8). But Constantia instead pities him. She tells him his love for Agnes is as hopeless as her own love for him. She says she loves him and Agnes equally, so she of all people can feel how compelling it is to love Agnes. Constantia does not say how she knows his love for Agnes is hopeless.

While Trotter is true to her source throughout Act I, she carefully shapes her scenes to intensify the relationship between the two women. In Act II, Trotter focuses on Alvaro's intimate relationship with the King and their mutual desire to force Agnes to marry Alvaro. In Behn's version, the King commands Agnes to marry Alvaro, to which she answers, "But, Sir, by what obstinate Power would you that I should love, if Heaven has not given me a Soul that is tender? And why should you pretend that I should submit to him, when nothing is dearer to me than my liberty?" Trotter's blank verse version reads as follows:

> **Agnes:** I question not Alvaro's merit, Sir,
> Nor have condemn'd him, though I have refus'd;
> But Heav'n, who ordain'd soft Mutual Love,
> A stronger tye of Souls than Marriage Vows,
> Had surely given me a Heart more tender,
> If 'twere design'd for such a Union;

I feel no melting, no soft Passion there;
None but for charming Liberty, and Glory;
Then Sir, wou'd you controul the Will of Heav'n
Who made me not for Love? (p. 13).

This is an interesting passage, for like Behn's Agnes, Trotter's character shows no signs of heterosexual interest. Behn says Agnes "found nothing" in Don Pedro, "but his being Husband to Constantia, that was dear to her." But Agnes lavishes kisses, embraces, tears, and protestations of great and lasting love on Constantia. Trotter's Agnes obviously knows something about "soft mutual love," "melting," and "soft Passion." Yet she says the "will of Heav'n" made her "not for love."

It seems likely that Behn and Trotter intended to communicate to their audiences that Agnes was excusing herself from marriage to Alvaro on the grounds that she was a lesbian. And evidence that Catharine Trotter would also fit that definition lends weight to this interpretation, and to an understanding of the characterization of the women in Trotter's play.

In 1688, the year Behn's *Agnes* was published in London, there also appeared in England *A Dialogue Between a Married Lady and a Maid,* which was, according to Lillian Faderman, primarily a translation of Chorier's *Satyra Sotadica,* a pornographic novel in which two women engage in sex as a prelude to heterosexual lovemaking.[6]

In a time when it was neither financially possible nor socially acceptable for any but the very wealthiest women to choose a life together, and when marriage was a contractual matter involving property and inheritance more than love or affection, lesbians—that is, women who loved each other—were almost universally married to men. If they were lucky, if one married a very rich man, the other might go along as a companion.

The relationship of Agnes to Constantia in Behn's novel, as in Trotter's play, fits that pattern. It also fits the definition of "lesbian" according to Faderman:

a relationship in which two women's strongest emotions and affections are directed toward each other.

Sexual contact may be a part of the relationship to a greater or lesser degree, or it may be entirely absent. By preference the two women spend most of their time together and share most aspects of their lives with each other.[7]

Although a study of lesbians and lesbianism in the late 17th century exceeds the scope of this paper, substantial evidence exists that such women as Katherine Phillips, Sarah Egerton, Lady Mary Chudleigh, Mary Astell, Elizabeth Elstob, and many other prominent women of the 17th and early 18th centuries, including Queen Anne herself, were lesbian according to the Faderman definition.[8] Therefore, there was in 1696 an audience of intellectual, fashionable, powerful lesbians to support and encourage the work of writers such as Catherine Trotter. The irony in her play, which those women would have recognized, is that none of the male characters acknowledges the significance of the women's attachment. Alvaro and the King persistently suspect Agnes of attempting to seduce Don Pedro. Alvaro assumes that he can win Agnes. Don Pedro, full of his own thoughts, does not even consider that Agnes might reject him. The only person in the play who trusts Agnes is Constantia. It is easy to imagine the knowing chuckles of the ladies in the boxes at Drury Lane.

A clue to Trotter's lesbianism, again using Faderman's definition as baseline, lies in Trotter's autobiography, *Olinda's Adventures,* in which she describes her agreement to marry:

> I had no Aversion for him, and since my Circumstances wou'd oblige me to Marry, and that I knew I could never love any Man; I thought it might as well be he as any other.[9]

In one of Delariviere Manley's key-novels, Manley portrays Trotter as a member of the fashionable lesbian clique which included some of Queen Anne's closest associates.[10] Manley knew Trotter well, as they were two of the so-called "Female Wits" maligned in a misogynistic play of 1697, and Manley wrote a commendatory poem which was published with the text of *Agnes,* a poem in which Manley salutes Trotter for being a spiritual descendent of Sappho.

Given Trotter's inclinations, then, the lesbian theme in Behn's translation of the French novel would have caught Trotter's eye; and in turn the audience of her time would have understood what she was doing in her play. Trotter took those undercurrents in Behn's work even further than Behn had and created an Agnes who is revolted by or indifferent to men and who saves all her passion for Constantia.

After Constantia's death in the play, Trotter's Agnes, departing from Behn's, says such things as "There's nothing vertuous, since Constantia's gone,/No Life without her" (p.31); speaking of her own impending death, Agnes says, "But I shall meet my Princess where I go,/And our unspotted Souls, in Bliss above,/Will know each other, and again will love" (p.34). Trotter's Agnes does *not* marry Don Pedro, despite his pleas for her to. She dies just before the final curtain, stabbed to death by Alvaro.

Catharine Trotter was only 17 years old when *Agnes de Castro* was produced at Drury Lane. Yet she was already a practiced writer, and already in the habit of helping support her mother and sister by writing.[11] She obviously understood the essentials of playwriting, as she skillfully adapted her text to dramatic treatment and provided roles which the actors of her day must have been delighted to portray. Besides, she needed the money.

As Edmund Gosse points out, "There is frequent reference to money in Catharine Trotter's writings, and the lack of it was the rock upon which her gifts were finally wrecked."[12] Indeed, from all the evidence of her life, it is clear that she married Patrick Cockburn for financial reasons, and that her subsequent life as a clergyman's wife was intellectually barren by comparison with her youth. In a letter to Alexander Pope written the year before she died, she recalls that she was once well-known to London literati:

> But they are all gone before me, though I was in a manner dead long before them. You had but just begun to dawn upon the world, when I retired from it.

Being married in 1708 I bid adieu to the muses, and so wholly gave myself up to the cares of a family, and the education of my children, that I scarce knew whether there was any such thing as books, plays, or poems stirring in Great Britain.[13]

Trotter had at least four children, three of whom survived her.

Mitford's *Inez de Castro* (1841)[14]

The circumstances of Mitford's play are somewhat different from those of Trotter's. As the play begins, Constance is patiently waiting for her contracted marriage to Don Pedro to take place. She has been waiting for months while Don Pedro has found reasons to postpone their wedding. In fact, Don Pedro is secretly already married to Inez de Castro. Don Pedro knows, as Inez does not, that an ancient law holds that if anyone "being a subject born" weds the heir to the kingdom, she must be put to death. Inez, a commoner, fits that description. Don Manuel, first minister to the King, wants to marry Inez, but she has rejected his proposals. As the play opens, D'Aquilac, a minister of the Spanish court of Constance's father, arrives in Lisbon to demand that the marriage of Constance and Pedro be performed and consummated, and further to remind King Alphonso that if the marriage does not take place, Alphonso will have broken his royal pact with Constance's father, whereby as a result war will ensue. Manuel wants the contracted marriage to take place so he can press for Inez's hand; D'Aquilac is there to defend Constance's honor and to try to avert war.

Constance and Inez do not appear on stage together until Act II, a scene in the forest during a deer hunt. Constance's first words to Inez in the play characterize their relationship throughout: "Begone! I need thee not." And a couple of lines later, "Have I not said begone?" (p. 7).

The principal action of Mitford's play is the pursuit by D'Aquilac and Manuel of the contracted marriage of Con-

stance and Don Pedro, the planned forced marriage of
Inez to Manuel, and the enforcement by King Alphonso of
the laws of the land. Mitford's play, then, is more about
the clash of human sentiment with law and order than
about love or relationships.

As the King and Manuel are about to force Inez into big-
amy, for she can't confess her marriage to Don Pedro without
breaking her promise to him, she implores Constance:

> Listen, lady,
> For very womanhood, We are of one age,
> One country, and one sex; defenseless women!
> . . . Oh, shall we not be true
> To one another? Save me! Save me! Once
> Thou lovedst thine own poor handmaid! (p. 12)

But Constance replies coldly, "On to the chapel!"

Don Pedro arrives in the nick of time, saves Inez from
the altar, and confesses they are married. Constance curses
them with "War and death,/Famine and pestilence; hate,
fiercest hate,/And bitter, bitter love" (p. 13). From this
point on the play is about the conflict between father, who
must enforce the law and execute Inez, and son, who wants
an exception made. In the end Inez stabs herself to death
to free Don Pedro from his problems and to make peace in
the family.

Silly though that may sound to modern ears, peace in the
family was an important issue to Mary Mitford. She never
married but supported a father whom she regarded as a god,
despite the fact that he gambled, drank, and generally
squandered all her earnings.[15] Mitford's closest relationship,
other than with her father, was with Elizabeth Barrett (later
Browning). The two women were at the height of their intimacy at the very time *Inez* had its premiere in London.[16]
They exchanged locks of hair, Mitford sent Barrett flowers,
they addressed each other as "beloved," "dearest," "dar-
ling." They later broke off their friendship when Barrett ran
off to marry Browning, which she revealed to Mitford only
after the event.[17] In fact Mitford, unable to define her feelings for Barrett within acceptable terms, described them in
familial and heterosexual images, writing to Barrett:

> My love and ambition for you often seems to be more like that of a mother for a son, or a father for a daughter (the two fondest of natural emotions) than the common bonds of even a close friendship between two women of different ages and similar pursuits . . . It is a strange feeling, but one of indescribable pleasure.[18]

Curiously, Mitford and Barrett do not mention the production of *Inez* in their letters. The letter Barrett wrote Mitford after the premiere of the play was entirely devoted to the dog Flush, which Mitford gave Barrett as a gift and about whom Virginia Woolf was later to write her charming mock-biography. While Mitford did not choose to present a model of female friendship onstage in 1841, she was experiencing what may have been the nearest thing to a passionate relationship with a woman, or with anyone, which she ever experienced—this while the play was being produced.

Clearly something had changed in the London air since the time of Trotter's play. Not only had lesbianism ceased to be fashionable; it has ceased, one would think, to exist at all. One scholar notes Mitford excelled in producing the kind of sentimentality and reinforcement of societal values which the public of her time heartily enjoyed.[19] An affectionate biographer said her work was "commonplace," but "in the same pleasant sense in which sweet fresh air and primroses, and cowslips, and the meadow-sweet she loved, are commonplace."[20] Like Trotter's, Mitford's life was a sad tale of genteel poverty and the urgent need to earn money from her writings. Mitford dared not introduce even a hint of lesbianism into her work, which leads to some considerations of the changes in audience between Trotter's time and Mitford's.

DISCUSSION

Increasingly from 1696 to 1841, women onstage loved each other less and competed with each other more. A comparison of these two plays offers a vivid example of a trend which may be observed in the progression, say, from

Aphra Behn to Hannah Cowley, and from Cowley to
Elizabeth Inchbald, Joanna Baillie, or the Michael Fields,
a lesbian couple who wrote very male-identified plays early
in the 20th century. Women playwrights up to Mrs. Inchbald's time were suspected of moral aberration anyway,[21]
for while it is one thing to write a novel in which women
embrace, it is quite another thing to ask two actresses to
embrace in front of an audience. As Judith Barlow notes in
her study of American women playwrights:

> In both content and form, drama tends to be a conser-
> vative medium. Readers and critics are more willing to
> accept new ideas and daring innovations when they
> are safely hidden between the covers of books, to be
> consumed in private, than when they are presented on
> the public stage.[22]

A tightening up of patriarchal suppression of women may
also be indicated. Lawrence Stone, in his massive study, *The
Family, Sex, and Marriage in England 1500-1800*, carefully
documents the development between Trotter's and Mitford's time of the "Closed Domesticated Nuclear Family,"
which was "bound together by strong affective ties."[23] A
result of this was that "Friends, neighbours and relatives all
receded into the background as the conjugal family turned
more in upon itself."[24] Trotter wrote at the close of the 17th
century, when extended kinship ties were already shrinking
but when it would not have been unusual for an aristocratic
lady to take a female friend to whom she was passionately
attached into her new marital home with her. But by Mitford's time the closed nuclear family did not open itself to
possibilities for a ménage à trois. In addition, as forced
marriage became less the norm, the same-sex confidante
couple of the Restoration stage gave way to the romantic
opposite-sex couple of 19th century melodrama.
    Trotter created a lesbian heroine at the crest of a wave of
feminism which "built a new understanding of women as a
group, intellectually equal to men but socially and politically
separate from them."[25] Mitford created a self-sacrificing,
devoted, heterosexual wife in a social context in which the
ideal heroine was "pious, passive, and beautiful."[26] One

implication of this comparison is that the 17th century offers a historical period especially ripe for the study of lesbian history and literature. It seems to have been a period in which, at least among affluent women, intimate relationships between women were viewed as attractive and could be presented artistically as ennobling and significant. Additional study of the period between Trotter and Mitford may yield anwers to important questions.

For if, at some fairly clear point in English history, significant relationships between women disappeared from the stage, then by studying this process we may learn more about: (1) the power of audience to influence what aspects of her own reality a lesbian artist may choose to reveal in her work; (2) the power of art to shape lesbian reality by affirming or denying the beauty of lesbian relationships; and, (3) the power of those who control the theatres, or, in our day the media, to affirm or deny lesbian existence by deciding which images of women are to be revealed to the general public.

NOTES

1. Studies of treatments of the legend include H. Th. Heinermann's *Ignez de Castro; die dramatischen Behandlungen der Sage in den Romanischen Literaturen* (Leipzig: Borna, 1914); Alfonso Lopes Vieira's *Ines de Castro na Poesia e na Lenda* (Alcobaca Festival publication, 1913); a thesis at Vitoria University in Spain written in 1904 by Angel Apraiz y Buesa called "D. Ines de Castro en el teatro castellano," and more recently a study by Suzanne Cornil entitled *Ines de Castro: Contribution a l'etude du developpement litteraire du theme dans les litteratures romanes* (Bruxelles: Palais des Academies, 1952); and a thesis in 1966 at the University of Texas at Austin by John Philip Farrance called "A Comparison of Velez de Guevara's *Reinar Despues de Morir* with Henri de Montherlant's *La Reine Morte.*"

2. Cornil, pp. 35–38.

3. *The life of Mary Russell Mitford: Told by herself in letters to her friends,* ed. A. G. K. L'Estrange (New York: Harper & Brothers, 1870), p. 68.

4. Quotations from Behn's translation in this paper are taken from the edition edited by Montague Summers, which appears in Vol. 5 of *The works of Aphra Behn* (New York: Benjamin Blom, 1915, reprinted 1967), pp. 211–256.

5. Quotations from the play are taken from the 1696 edition "Printed for H. Rhodes in Fleetstreet."

6. *Surpassing the love of men: Romantic friendship and love between women from the renaissance to the present* (New York: William Morrow, 1981), pp. 17–18.

7. Faderman, p. 74.

8. See especially Hilda Smith, *Reason's disciples: Seventeenth century English feminists* (Urbana: University of Illinois Press, 1982); and Joan K. Kin-

naird, "Mary Astell: Inspired by ideas," In *Feminist theorists* (New York: Pantheon, 1983).

9. Catharine (Trotter) Cockburn, *Olinda's adventures; or, The amours of a young lady* (Los Angeles: William A. Clark Memorial Library, 1969 facsimile reprint of 1718 edition), p. 189.

10. In *Memoirs of the new Atalantis,* included in *The novels of Mary Delariviere Manley,* facsimile reprint edited with an introduction by Patricia Koster (Gainesville, Florida: Scholars Facsimile Reprints, 1971), pp. 587–588.

11. A biography of Catharine Trotter by Thomas Birch appears in his edition of her *Works* (London: Printed for J. & P. Knapton, 1751).

12. "Catharine Trotter, the Precursor of the Bluestockings," in *Transactions of the Royal Society of Literature of the U.K.,* Vol. XXXIV (London: Oxford University Press, 1916), p. 90.

13. Quoted by Birch, p. xl.

14. Quotations from the play are taken from the published edition, No. 672 of *Dick's Standard Plays,* printed in London with a cast list from the April 12, 1841, production.

15. Sources of information on Mary Russell Mitford are numerous, for the most part consistent, and include over 15 volumes of published letters, 6 book-length biographies, and a revealing reflected portrait which emerges from the published letters of Elizabeth Barrett (later Browning) to Mitford. All emphasize her intense relationship with her father.

16. Elizabeth Barrett Browning, *Elizabeth Barrett to Miss Mitford,* ed. Betty Miller (London: John Murray, 1954), see especially p. xv, Mitford quoted saying, "Next to my father, she is the one I love best."

17. Browning, pp. x–xv.

18. Browning, p. 72.

19. Lynne Agress, *The feminine irony: Women on women in early-nineteenth-century English literature* (Rutherford, NJ: Fairleigh Dickinson University Press, 1978), p. 138.

20. Helen Gray Cone, "Mary Russell Mitford," in *Pen-portraits of literary women,* ed. Cone and Jeannette Gilder (New York: Cassell, 1887), p. 271.

21. Agress, pp. 138–139.

22. In the introduction to *Plays by American women: The early years* (New York: Avon, 1981), p. xiii.

23. (New York: Columbia University Press, 1980), p. 412–413.

24. Stone, p. 397.

25. Smith's *Reason's disciples,* cited above, p. 16.

26. Agress, p. 176.

Love Between Women in 1928: Why Progressivism Is Not Always Progress

Lillian Faderman, PhD

California State University, Fresno

ABSTRACT. Because lesbianism, as described by sexologists of the late 19th and early 20th centuries, was treated overtly in a number of novels of the 1920s, while earlier literature seemed seldom to recognize its existence, it appeared that what had been a taboo subject suddenly "came out of the closet" in a liberal and sophisticated era. In fact, fiction of earlier eras often dealt with love between women in the most romantic and positive terms. The fiction of the 1920s was no more frank about affection between women than its predecessors, but it differed from earlier work by depicting women who loved other women as congenitally abnormal, neurotic, peculiar, or outcast. These changes in the literary view of love between women came about because the spread of sexology "wisdom" created a hitherto seldom acknowledged category of abnormality. Women's increasing economic independence opened the possibility of permanence in such relationships, posing an ostensible threat to heterosexuality. And the new interest in companionate marriage encouraged heterosociality and heterosexuality as it had not been encouraged before, to the exclusion of love between women.

In his 1928 preface to *The Well of Loneliness,* Havelock Ellis described Radclyffe Hall's book as "the first English novel which presents, in a completely faithful and uncompromising form," a study of love between women.[1] In that same year a number of other fairly explicit novels dealing with lesbianism were also published. It would have seemed to the casual observer in the late 1920s that what had hith-

---

Dr. Faderman is a professor of English at California State University, Fresno. She is the author of *Surpassing the Love of Men, Scotch Verdict,* and numerous articles on homosexual relationships. Reprint requests may be sent to the author, English Department, California State University, Fresno, Fresno, CA 93740. This paper was presented at the conference, *Among Men, Among Women,* at the University of Amsterdam, June 1983.

erto been a taboo subject was finally, thanks to modern frankness, being treated openly.

By then, as I have observed elsewhere,[2] widespread acceptance of love between women, as manifested in the institutions of romantic friendship and Boston marriage, was long since dead. Only the rare literary historian would have been familiar with fiction such as Charles Brockden Brown's *Ormond,* Louisa May Alcott's *Work,* Florence Converse's *Diana Victrix,* and Sarah Orne Jewett's *Martha's Lady.* Those works, too, may be said to describe love between women in a "completely faithful" form. But unlike Hall's Stephen Gordon, the women characters of those novels never consider themselves abnormal or pathetic because they love other women. Those 18th and 19th century fictional studies were free of the later influences that placed what had long been recognized as normal emotion into the realm of the morbid and the rebellious.

A half dozen fictional works dealing with love between women, by authors of some renown, were published in 1928: Hall's *The Well of Loneliness,* Compton Mackenzie's *Extraordinary Women,* Djuna Barnes's *Ladies Almanack,* Wanda Fraiken Neff's *We Sing Diana,* Elizabeth Bowen's *The Hotel,* and Virginia Woolf's *Orlando.* They all demonstrate, to a greater or lesser extent, that science, sexual revolutions, and liberalism sometimes bring about a specious progress. These works depict love between women as it was seldom depicted before in modern history. They create the fictional lesbian: not a woman who was expressing emotion quite within the realm of the normal, but rather an outcast, a neurotic, a peculiarity.

To be brief, since I have discussed most of these works in *Surpassing the Love of Men,* each one presents a largely negative view of love between women.[3] Radclyffe Hall was torn in her creation of Stephen Gordon (*The Well of Loneliness*) between explaining female homosexual love in the terms of the congenitalists, who claimed that an invert was born with her peculiarity, and the Freudians, who said that the lesbian was produced by childhood trauma. As her research notes[4] and her request to Havelock Ellis to write a preface indicate, she leaned finally towards the congenitalists. But although love between women is explained in her novel as being primarily a problem of having been born into the third sex, it is accompanied by devastating disorders. Hall refers, for example, to "the terrible nerves of the invert, those nerves that are always lying in wait, [that grip] like live wires through her body, causing a constant and ruthless torment"[5] and to "those haunted, tormented eyes of the invert."[6]

In Wanda Fraiken Neff's *We Sing Diana,* a novel which focuses on an American women's college, love between women is described as "this poison," and Nora, the heroine, witnessing two girls kissing has "a sick memory of the fungi she had studied in botany, the rank growths, forms of life springing up in unhealthy places, feeding on rot." She then observes, "Creation wasn't all clean and pure. Nor human relationships."[7] This novel is especially interesting because it suggests the rise of Freudian consciousness in the 1920s. Nora is first seen at college as a student in 1913. At that time all the freshmen are openly in love with Miss Goodwin, a young professor, and with each other. After World War I, in the 1920s, Nora returns to teach in the same college, where everyone is talking about psychoanalysis, and "the exchange of undergraduate speech was full of psychological tags." Love between women is viewed with a suspicion that was uncommon in the previous decade in America: "Intimacies between girls were watched with keen, distrustful eyes. Among one's classmates, one looked for the bisexual type, the masculine girl searching for a feminine counterpart, and one ridiculed their devotions."

In *The Hotel,* Elizabeth Bowen depicts the same ubiquitous awareness of the morbidity of homosexual love, which was generally absent from earlier English and American literature. "These very violent friendships" between women are described by one character as "not quite healthy." Another states, "I should discourage any daughter of mine from a friendship with an older woman. It is never the best women who have these strong influences. I would far rather she lost her head about a man."[8] Love between women is viewed here as flawed at best. It is either characterized by manipulativeness and coldness, or where it appears to be idyllic, characterized as foolish. For example, two women characters who are pictured at the conclusion as "hand in hand, reunited, in perfect security" are seen both early and late in the book as quibbling with each other and losing patience over trifles. Bowen thus "ridicules their devotions," as Neff observes to be common in a psychoanalytically "aware" society.

Djuna Barnes's *Ladies Almanack,* which was privately printed and intended primarily for the author's own circle of lesbian friends, shows that even women who loved women in the 1920s internalized the theories of the sexologists, to the point that they could not explain their love as a normal emotion such as their earlier counterparts might have. Even as depicted by lesbian writers in the 1920s, love between women had abnormal causes, and women who loved women during that time were seen to behave like men. When Evangeline's father laments that he perceives in her masculine sentiments, she responds, apparently explaining the genesis as well as the fact of her homosexuality, "Thou, good Governor, wast expecting a Son when you lay atop of your Choosing; why then be so mortal wounded when you perceive that you have your Wish? Am I not doing after your very Desire, and is it nor more commendable, seeing that I do without the Tools for the Trade, and yet nothing complain?"[9] Love between women here is clearly and specifically genital, as compared to the diffuse eroticism and homoaffectionality that was reflected in the literature of other eras. But while it sometimes appears that Barnes believes a woman is born lesbian, at other times she indicates an acceptance of psychoanalytic theories, such as those which explain lesbianism as a form of narcissim. For example, comparing heterosexual and homosexual love, Maisie Tuch-and-Frill, who seems to be a persona for Barnes proclaims, "A man's love is built to fit Nature. Woman's is a Kiss in the Mirror."[10]

Compton Mackenzie's *Extraordinary Women* illustrates yet another explanation for love between women: It is the result of World War I. Rosalba, the young lesbian of his satirical novel, explains during the war years, "I am not at all interested in men . . . They have let themselves be enslaved too easily by this war. I have lost my respect for men."[11] Because men went off to the trenches, Mackenzie suggests, some females had to fill their places. Therefore,

Rosalba, who is a "pretty young woman," tries "to dress and behave as much like a handsome young man as she could." Mackenzie's is a cautionary tale. This is what happens if men make war instead of love and force women to carry on civilization without them. By the 1920s, because men had forfeited female respect and thus driven women to independence, Rosalba, Mackenzie says, "would cease to be a precursor and . . . her boyishness would presently be blurred by myriads of post-war girls affecting boyishness."[13] The rest of the lesbian characters, all of them more or less ridiculous (peculiar fauna, as Mackenzie calls them), make it clear that while he sees the cause of lesbianism and feminism as male neglect, he does not excuse the women who have chosen such ludicrous paths.

Because love between women had fallen into such disrepute by 1928, Virginia Woolf could not treat the bisexuality of Vita Sackville-West, who became her Orlando, with honesty.[14] She had intended to write a lesbian novel just before she embarked on *Orlando.* Her diary for March 14, 1927, referred to a "fantasy" she was working on called *The Jessamy Brides,* which she wrote was to deal with "Sapphism."[15] Some months later she began *Orlando,* but in her diary on December 20th she admitted regarding that book, "I see looking back just now to March that it is almost exactly in spirit, though not in actual facts, the book I planned then."[16] However, *Orlando* deals not with Sapphism, as Woolf had originally intended, but rather with androgyny and sex changes. Once Woolf decided to model her central character on a living person (and a friend), she could not treat love between women except in a very disguised form.[17]

In fact, homosexual love is depicted often as not existing in the realm of this novel. Although Woolf does say that while in Constantinople the male Orlando "became the adored of many women and some men,"[18] much more typically she denies such possibilities. For example, when the male Orlando first sees the appealing figure of Sasha, he despairs lest it be a boy. If Sasha is a boy, the narrator observes, "all embraces were out of the question."[19] In the 19th century Orlando becomes primarily female, yet she enjoys "the love of both sexes equally." Here Woolf is

perhaps purposely ambiguous. One who is apparently female can enjoy the love of both sexes only by becoming
male from time to time, but it is not clear if maleness refers
merely to costume, as it often did in Vita Sackville-West's
lesbian exploits, or if costume indicates changed gender, as
it generally does in this novel. In any case, Woolf explains
that Orlando can enjoy the love of both males and females
because she (or he) is sometimes one who wears breeches
and sometimes one who wears petticoats.[20] However, that
one in petticoats might love another in petticoats is never
acknowledged.

All these depictions of women who love women as congenital inverts, neurotics, products of a failed civilization,
as well as the likes of Woolf's disguised depiction which
largely denied her subject's bisexuality, were seldom to be
found in English and American Fiction before World War
I.[21] What were the social and intellectual forces which resulted in these attitudes towards love between women?
And why did they reach an apogee in 1928?

I suggested in *Surpassing the Love of Men* that as a
result of the 19th and early 20th century feminist movement, women gradually gained significant economic and
social independence. Romantic friendships, which might
have been viewed as harmless to the heterosexual status
quo, thus became increasingly threatening since many
women no longer had to marry for the sake of economic
and social survival alone. Romantic friendships could potentially take the place of marriage on a scale much larger
than what had before been possible.

In addition, the spread of the theories of late-
19th-century sexologists created a category of abnormality
for women who loved women; what had once been widely
viewed as normal became peculiar. Many women learned
that they loved other women only because they suffered
from some hereditary taint. Therefore, they needed to repress such emotions lest they cause embarrassment, pain, or
worse to their families and themselves. While these pressures began to be felt in the late 19th century, they were
apparently ignorable for many until after World War I. But
as the spate of novels such as those I have discussed indicates, a decade after the war almost no one continued to

believe that romantic friendship was harmless to the fabric of society. The lesbian became a well-known category of sexual deviance and an outcast. One writer who was born in 1896 observed in an article written in the late 1920s that the happy innocence of her youth with regard to the "evils" of homosexual love had, "unfortunately" she wrote, disappeared and had been replaced in the 1920s by the pressure on young people to express themselves heterosexually, whether they wanted to or not. When she was young, the writer recalled, "there still remained a genuine and important outlet for eroticism, without any guilty attachment," in the expression of love young females were permitted to offer each other. However, in the 1920s she observed, there had been "a growth in half-knowledge which makes all girlish fondness suspect, so that the door is shut on these minor 'innocent' outlets . . . or else it is opened wide on the horrendous and fascinating."[22]

While in the 19th century many anti-feminist writers attacked women who agitated for independence by calling them unfeminine,[23] by the 1920s it became acceptable to hurl at such women a more dramatic and frightening epithet: They were lesbians—and that explained their lack of feminine passivity and contentment. The increasing popularization of Sigmund Freud's theories throughout the 1920s,[24] and particularly the translation at the beginning of that decade of his essay on lesbianism, "The Psychogenesis of a Case of Homosexuality in a Woman," made the existence of female homosexuality common knowledge, as it apparently had not been in England and America in earlier eras.

According to writers of the 1920s who promulgated a popular application of Freud, the most important touchstone by which it could be determined whether a child was "growing up" was by observing whether he or she was "becoming more fully heterosexual."[25] And the only way for society to emerge from its "welter of neuroticism" was to accept "the full and passionate love of the other sex as the normal goal of youth."[26] Heterosexuality thus became "mental hygiene" modeled after Freud's discoveries, his followers claimed.

However, it was widely feared during this time that fe-

male homosexuality, which as a result of Freud's disciples
was no longer thought to be congenital, but rather the
result of environmental influences, was rapidly increasing.
Many psychologists and sociologists claimed the increase
was due to what the modern woman had been permitted to
become. Mathilde and Mathias Vaertig pointed out in 1924
that the secondary sex characteristics were by then so
modified that differentiation between the sexes was significantly decreasing. The women of the 1920s, they lamented,
were developing boyish figures, athletic skills, executive
abilities, and were meeting with professional success. Even
so, women of the 1920s could not approximate the conventional masculine ideal as easily as they could be feminine.[27]
It was feared that the "masculinization" of the female
threatened the institution of heterosexuality. Masculinization created women with strong personalities who, according to Dr. Phyllis Blanchard in 1929, found satisfaction in
guiding and protecting weaker women. That, she said,
could result in the "grave danger" that both strong and
weak women would be "unable to adjust to the more natural relationship" of heterosexuality.[28] English and American doctors, female as well as male, expressed alarm at
"the increasing role which homosexuality is coming to play
in the life of the modern girl." Some claimed in the most
Freudian terms that it was "the failure to transfer the libido from a love object of the same sex to one of the
opposite sex, which is responsible in part for the increasing
number of women celibates and divorces,"[29] and that the
driving force in many agitators and militant women who
were always after their rights was often unsatisfied homosexual impulses. Married women with a completely satisfied libido would rarely take an active interest in militant
movements.[30]

In America by 1920, almost half the college population
was female (238,000) and over 8,600,000 women were
working at paying jobs in diverse areas. It could no longer
be stated, as the English writer Harriet Martineau said of
the American women she observed several decades before,
that "middle class women who wished to work could do
nothing but teach school or sew."[31] The result of this sud-
den proliferation of independent women caused violent re-

actions, as evidenced in the pages of popular magazines. Sidney Ditzion, author of *Marriage, Morals, and Sex in America,* points out that one response of the popular magazine was simply to pretend that the new woman didn't exist. Although women had gone through radical transformations, on many popular magazine covers they still retained their old look. They were depicted just as they had been in other decades, holding mirrors, fans, flowers, or babies.[32]

On the other hand, many magazine articles confronted the disturbing issue of the independent woman head-on. *Harpers* was one magazine that ran numerous articles during the 1920s about the effect of the "New Woman" on the American way of life. A 1928 article, "This Two-Headed Monster—The Family," pointed out that the divorce rate was so high because of "the new independent ways of American women, who have come to believe that they can win arguments by assertiveness rather than seduction." The author expressed his anger that "public opinion permits the American wife to make money whether or not it is really needed." He blamed the women's movement, which he tried to discredit by suggesting that it would be the ruin of the family.[33]

In another *Harpers* article which appeared the following year, "A Case of Two Careers," the writer observed that he knew 14 other marriages besides his own in which the wives were pursuing independent careers. The 28 people in those marriages had managed to produce only 7 children. But even worse, as he discovered himself, a woman's pursuit of a career brings about destruction of the men in her life. In his own case, he witnessed the disappearance of all his wife's "womanly" qualities, developed an "inferiority complex," took to drinking, ruined his own career, and finally realized that the only solution to his problems was to get rid of his working wife.[34]

Such cautionary tales which appeared throughout the 1920s may well have had some effect on the decline in female ambitions by the end of that decade. A 1924 study of young women indicated that 61% "reported a career as the thing they would select, if they could choose anything in the world," while only 39% "preferred to be wives and mothers." Five years later, a study of a comparable group of young women showed that only 13% preferred a career to marriage, 38% wished to combine the two, and the rest preferred to be wives and mothers.[35]

It is apparent that many people found female independence extremely disturbing during the 1920s. Since lesbianism had been associated with the desire for independence, and since the sexologists had made it clear that love between women was not normal, to accuse a woman who wanted to be independent of lesbianism was a logical ploy for those who preferred the status quo. It was also logical that the public should welcome explicit discussion of lesbianism in literature as long as that discussion showed love between women to be unhappy and abnormal. Here then would be a clear demonstration of the dangers concomitant with being a new woman.

But there is still another explanation which accounts for the negative views of love between women in 1928: the sexual revolution. By the mid-1920s, contraceptive devices became widely available as a result of Margaret Sanger's Birth Control Clinical Research Center, and birth control clinics had multiplied rapidly. Therefore, the fear of pregnancy, which had been seen as the great danger in premarital sex and which had served as a restraint, probably for men as well as women, was gone. A man could more reasonably—or less outrageously—demand that a woman not place limits on the degree of intimacy in which she would indulge with him. Sexual, or rather heterosexual, Puritanism, became passé. Popular arguments from Freud assisted this revolution. If a woman refuses to be "receptive" to a man, she was repressing a natural urge, blocking her libido, and that would make her neurotic. In *The Natural History of Love,* Morton Hunt observes that the leaders of this sexual revolution "sometimes accomplished the almost impossible task of making pleasure seem like medical necessity."[36]

The automobile, which was affordable by many in the 1920s, became another aid to the (hetero)sexual revolution. In *We Sing Diana,* Wanda Neff discusses the increase in heterosociality among college women that was made possible by the automobile. When her character Nora had

been a student before World War I, suitors were rarely
seen around the campus of the women's college she attended, which was located away from a city. Males visited
the campus only for rare events such as proms. At other
times, Nora observes, "one had peace."[37] Then, in the
1920s, when Nora returns to the college as a professor, she
discovers that young men of the middle class all have cars.
If a girl doesn't have a swain picking her up for a date her
"failure to attract men" is "advertised," and that failure
affects her popularity among the other students.

While in past decades it had often been impossible for an
unmarried man and woman to manage privacy together in
the parlor, where a member of her family might intrude at
any moment, in the 1920s the automobile could take a
couple miles away from her family. "Petting" became an
expected behavior on a date; dating became the "raison
d'être" of flaming youth and flapper. Ben Lindsey, a 1920s
family court judge and co-author of *The Revolt of Modern
Youth,* estimated, unscientifically but with assurance of his
accuracy based on extensive anecdotal evidence, that more
than 90% of those young people who rode together in
automobiles indulged in petting, and that 15 to 20% of that
90% "go the limit,"[38] an estimate which subsequent statistical research proved to be low.

Another social commentator in the 1920s, Lorine Pruette,
observed in her essay "The Flapper" that the "new compulsion to be 'free' " impelled many into (hetero)sexual relations without either the "instinct" or the "inclination." She
argued that the "older system," while perhaps hypocritical
and repressive, at least allowed individuals some chance of
living according to their own tempo and inclination. In past
generations, she pointed out, those who were most determined and most desirous could find ways to engage in sexual
adventures. But in the 1920s "whole groups appear to fall
under the suggestion that they must busy themselves with
flaming bright red when all they want is to be a mild and
more salubrious pink."[39] The 19th-century excesses of heterosexual repression, in the words of still another 1920s
sociologist, had been replaced by "the excess of (hetero)-
sexual expression."[40]

Thus, in the 1920s there was pressure to engage more

actively in heterosexuality, both socially and sexually. The double standard, as it related to sexual expression, was, if not outmoded, at least weakened. A woman, therefore, could not rely as readily on the hitherto acceptable excuse of "properness," of wishing to be a "good girl," if she wanted to refrain from heterosexuality. At least it appears that fewer women found that excuse efficacious or desirable in the 1920s than did their older counterparts. Women born in the late 19th century were much less likely to have premarital sexual intercourse than those born after 1900. For example, of those born before 1900 and still unmarried by the age of 25, only 14% had had heterosexual intercourse. Of their counterparts born in the next decade, i.e., those women who would have been in their 20's in the 1920s, 36% had had premarital intercourse by age 25, and of those remaining unmarried past 35, 60% had had intercourse, while only about half that number of their older counterparts had had intercourse by the same age.[41]

In her article "Companionate Marriage and the Lesbian Threat," Christina Simmons offers another explanation as to why love between women fell into disfavor in the 1920s. For a variety of reasons including women's increasing independence, companionate marriage, which sought to rectify the most oppressive elements of Victorian marriage and to make marriage "a bond of creative companionship and interdependent cooperation," became an ideal in the 1920s. Because "companionate" marriage was an expressed ideal, the tradition and social structures that separated the sexes came to appear as obstacles to heterosexual companionship and romance. This meant that women's segregation and their solidarity with each other, which had earlier been socially approved, now took on a menacing quality. This was heightened by the new admission that women were indeed sexual creatures. Since sexual relationships were seen as vital to women's happiness, in the 1920s love between women came to be suspected as sexual and, in a phallocentric definition, to be a result of the absence or failure of satisfactory heterosexual experience.[42]

Numerous marriage manuals and other books on how to achieve happiness published during this period pressured men to perform sexually, to bring their mates to orgasm and contentment.[43] If they were unsuccessful, the blame was attributed not only to their "performance skills," but also to the woman's failure to transfer the libido from a love object of the same sex to one of the opposite sex.[44] Since in earlier eras "decent" women were generally not expected to respond to men sexually, no such "explanations" for unresponsiveness were sought; thus, it would have been quite unlikely that lesbianism would have been suspected as a reason for heterosexual unhappiness.[45]

Fear of the ramifications of the feminists' success, the concomitant popularization of the theories of the sexologists, the sexual revolution and the concurrent availability of the automobile which pressured women to become more heterosocial and more heterosexually active, the idealization of companionate marriage—all of these factors help to account for the negative social attitudes towards love between women and their reflection in the fiction of 1928. But as the historian Carl Degler has pointed out in another context, there is sometimes a difference between "what ought to be" and "what was." It is true that public attitudes militated against love between women, but how did women behave when they were alone together?

The two studies which consider female homosexual relationships in the 1920s are Katherine Bement Davis's "Factors in the Sex Life of Twenty-Two-Hundred Women" (1929) and Gilbert Hamilton's "A Research in Marriage" (1929). Davis's study included both married and unmarried women, all of whom were assumed to be heterosexual when selected for interview. However, 50.4% of her sample indicated that they had experienced "intense emotional relations with other women." About 26% of the sample said that those relations were accompanied by sex or were "recognized as sexual in character."[46] These were not childhood experiences that most of the women were describing: 77% of those who had had "intense emotional relations" with other females, and 79% of those who recognized those relations as "sexual in character," had had their experiences when they were over 30 years of age."[47]

Hamilton's sample was smaller (only 100 women, all married), but his results appear to have been similar. This is somewhat surprising, since the statements with which he prefaced his questions to women regarding their lesbian experiences were quite negative, and may even have encouraged some women to suppress information about that aspect of their lives. For example, while he points out in his comments prefacing the questions that young girls often have crushes on other girls, he also states:

> A girl who has had such experiences with her girl chum (may) learn that there are perverted girls and women who make a regular practice of using girls or women as sex objects, and whose sex feelings are exclusively aroused and satisfied by persons of their own sex. The girl who finds this out may then be much terrified lest she be regarded as sexually unnatural in this respect. . .
>
> A girl, having found this out by "fooling" in one way or another with a girl or a woman (may grow) into womanhood with a strong tendency to love girls and women in a sexual way, and to have sex feelings for them rather than for men. Such a girl may carefully conceal her desires and preferences in the matter, or she may form a kind of sexual alliance with another person of her own sex. Cases of this kind are comparatively rare, but cases of girls and women who are really quite normal, but who have a morbid fear lest they feel sexually toward a person of the same sex, are quite common.
>
> Perhaps no woman reaches maturity without having experienced more or less discomfort from the thought that she may have a "holdover" from her girlhood in the form of an inclination towards girls and women as sex objects. Groundless fear of this aspect of human sex life probably does serious damage to a thousand personalities for every one personality with the actual development of the most feared tendency. It is therefore quite important that you have this part of your mental anatomy examined.[48]

Despite such descriptions as "the much feared tendency" regarding love between women, there were 43 positive responses to the question asking whether the women had had "crushes" on other females "not involving conscious sex elements" (although, significantly, the average age in which the "crush" occurred was much lower than in the Davis sample). There were 15 positive responses to the question asking whether they had experienced feeling for females "involving conscious sex attraction but not involving sex organ stimulation." But most astonishing, there were 31 positive responses among these married women to the question asking if they had experienced such attractions "which involved sex organ stimulation."[49] (N. B. Hamilton groups his responses by age of experience and does not indicate whether the groups are mutually exclusive. Therefore, 43 positive responses does not necessarily mean that 43% of the women admitted having had crushes on other females. Some of the women who responded positively may have had crushes while in more than one age group.) Most of those experiences (50) occurred after the age of 18, i.e., for the most part, these were not childhood experiments that were being described. Also, 27% of these married women admitted that even at the time of the study other women were attractive to them "in a sexual way."[51]

Since so large a number admitted to having experienced homosexual attraction at some time in their lives, on the surface it would appear that whatever bad press love between women had received during the 1920s, and however negative Hamilton's prefacing comments were, they had not substantially affected women's lives or their views of homosexual love. But another statistic in Hamilton's study is extremely revealing in this regard: 34% of the women admitted to being uncomfortable if another woman merely "put her arm" around the respondent or "made other physical demonstrations of friendliness."[52] The implication is obvious. Since women were taught from a myriad of sources that lesbianism was morbid, many of them responded as one might even to the slightest signs of morbidity, despite experiences which, if these women were like the women of Davis's sample, for the most part promoted health and happiness.[53]

There is also evidence that the growing social fear of homosexuality finally had a significant effect on women's lives after the period under consideration. Alfred Kinsey's study, "Sexual Behavior in the Human Female,"[54] shows the number of women who admitted to "psychological arousal" by another female to be substantially lower than the 1920 studies: only 28% of the Kinsey sample, compared to 50.4% of the Davis sample. There appears also to be fewer women who admitted to physical arousal in the 1953 study, although absolute comparison is difficult because the breakdown of figures is not as clear in Davis and Hamilton as it is in Kinsey. Of Kinsey's sample, 19% said they had homosexual physical contact "which was deliberately and consciously . . . intended to be sexual," and 13% said they had sexual contact to orgasm with other women.[55] Hamilton did not ask his respondents about orgasm, but he indicated 15 and 31 positive responses to questions regarding sexuality between women. Hamilton indicated 15 positive responses to the question of homosexual feeling "involving conscious sex attraction but not involving sex organ stimulation," and 31 positive responses to the question regarding homosexual attractions "which involved sex organ stimulation." (However, these figures do not necessarily indicate 15% and 31%, since the same women may have responded positively in several of the age group categories.) Davis placed 26% of the women in a category of those whose homosexual relations either involved sexual expression or were "recognized as sexual in character."

These figures, particularly those regarding psychological arousal, suggest that after the 1920s women were less likely to admit to, and perhaps engage in, affectional relations with other women. One would also venture to guess, however, that they were more likely to engage in specifically sexual activity together in the post-World War I decade than in earlier times, since women were told so insistently after the war that they were sexual creatures. Therefore, if they permitted themselves to experience a "homoaffectional" attachment, with increased "sophistication" regarding sexual matters, it was more likely that they would be forced to see the attachment as homosexual as well. But since female homosexuality had by then become a well-known category of sexual perversion, many women would be less likely to admit to "homoaffectionality."

Even casual, public behavior reflects the relatively new taboos regarding love between women. In the 19th century, a decent woman would never be seen kissing a man in public, though she might display all manner of affection towards another woman. In our era, which is generally considered so open-minded with regard to sexual matters, especially when compared to the previous century, a decent woman may certainly kiss a man in public, but she had better not display affection toward another female in public, such as holding hands with or sitting very close. If she does she will be considered queer, as the experiment conducted by the Palo Alto, California, school girls in 1973 indicated.[56] Relations between and within the sexes have reversed themselves. One taboo has been exchanged for another.

In 1798, Charles Brockden Brown allowed the very admirable female narrator of his novel *Ormond* to observe with regard to herself and her female friend: "I would not part from her side, but ate and slept, walked and mused and read, with my arm locked in hers, and with her breath fanning my cheek . . . O precious inebriation of the heart! O preeminent love!" And the two women live happily ever after together. A hundred years later, as reflected in Florence Converse's novel *Diana Victrix* (1897), very admirable heroines could still say the same sorts of things about each other and end by living happily ever after together. A few decades later, however, with the advent of "modern views," "sophistication," and the "sexual revolution," such happy utterances were no longer possible in fiction, and were probably made with difficulty or agony in real life. With regard to love between women, which for so long was a joyous and healthy possibility in women's lives, progressivism has not meant progress.

NOTES

1. Havelock Ellis, commentary on *The Well of Loneliness* (Garden City, NY: Blue Ribbon Books, 1928).

2. Lillian Faderman, *Surpassing the Love of Men* (New York: Morrow, 1981).

3. I disagree with Jeanette Foster (Sex Variant Women in Literature 1956;

rpt. Baltimore, Maryland: Diana Press, 1975, p. 287) who sees the "annual balance" of literature in 1928 as being "on the whole positive" regarding views of love between women.

4. In preparation for writing *The Well of Loneliness* Hall compiled a set of notes based on "the latest and revised editions of the works of the highest authorities on sexual inversion, exclusive of the psycho-analysts." Her "authorities" were all congenitalists, e.g., Havelock Ellis, Iwan Bloch, Magnus Hirschfeld. In Radclyffe Hall papers, Humanities Research Center, University of Texas, Austin, Texas.

5. *The Well of Loneliness,* p. 209.

6. Ibid., p. 477.

7. Wanda Fraiken Neff, *We Sing Diana* (Boston: Houghton Mifflin, 1928) p. 64.

8. Elizabeth Bowen, *The Hotel* (rpt. New York: Dial, 1928), p. 88.

9. Djuna Barnes, *Ladies Almanack* (1928; New York: Harper and Row, 1972) p. 8.

10. Ibid., p. 23.

11. Compton Mackenzie, *Extraordinary Women: Theme and Variations* (New York: Vanguard Press, 1928), p. 39.

12. Ibid., p. 41.

13. Ibid., p. 390.

14. Woolf and the Bloomsbury group were very aware of the sexologists views of homosexuality. Barbara Fassler "Theories of Homosexuality as sources for Bloomsbury's Androgyny," *Signs: Journal of Women in Culture and Society,* V, 2 (Winter 1979), 237–51, suggests that Bloomsbury was especially influenced by the congenitalists, although they were familiar with Freud. Virginia Woolf's Hogarth Press published the English editions of Freud. See also Surpassing pp. 366–68 for a discussion of Vita Sackville-West's internalization of the negative views of same-sex love.

15. Virgina Woolf, *A Writer's Diary* (New York: Harcourt Brace, 1953), p. 104.

16. Ibid., p. 118.

17. Woolf may have shared the ambivalence toward lesbianism that she attributes to Mrs. Dalloway who, although she regarded her relationship with Sally Seton as an emotional highlight of her life and "could not resist sometimes yielding to the charm of a woman," nevertheless "had a scruple picked up Heaven knows where, or, as she felt, sent by Nature (Who is invariably wise)," Virginia Woolf, *Mrs. Dalloway* (1925; rpt. New York: Harcourt Brace, 1953), p. 46.

18. Virginia Woolf, *Orlando* (1928; rpt. New York: Harcourt Brace, 1956), p. 125.

19. Ibid., p. 38.

20. Ibid., p. 221.

21. In my chapter "The Last Breath of Innocence" in *Surpassing,* I discuss numerous examples of pre-War twentieth century English and American fiction which depict love between women in those positive terms that were typical of the nineteenth century and earlier.

22. Lorine Pruette. "The Flapper," *The New Generation: The Intimate Problems of Modern Parents and Their Children,* eds V.F. Calverton and Samuel D. Schmalhausen (1930; rpt. New York: Arno Press, 1971), pp. 574–75.

23. See *surpassing,* pp. 235–36.

24. One indication of this popularization is in the magazines of the 1920's, which frequently carried articles that presented Freudianism for the masses, e.g., "How it Feels to be Psychoanalyzed," "Freud and Our Frailties," "A new Diagnosis for Hidden Mental Taint."

25. Floyd, Dell, *Love in the Machine Age* (1930; rpt. New York: Farrar, Straus, and Giroux, 1973), p. 282.

26. Ibid.

27. Mathilde and Mathias Vaertig, "Dominant Sexes," *Our Changing Morality*, ed. Freda Kirchwey (New York: Boni, 1924), pp. 147–63.

28. Phyllis Blanchard, "Sex in the Adolescent Girl," *Sex in Civilization*, eds. V.F. Calverton and Samuel D. Schmalhausen (Garden City, NY: Garden City Publishers, 1929), pp. 538–61.

29. Dr. Constance Long (English) and Dr. Eleanor Bertine (American), quoted in Floyd Dell, op. cit., p. 239.

30. John F.W. Meagher, "Homosexuality: Its Psychological and Psychopathological Significance," *Urologic and Cutaneous Review*, 33 (1929), 510.

31. Quoted in Mildred Adams, *The Right to Be People* (Phil.: J.B. Lippincott, 1967), pp. 189–90.

32. Sidney Ditzion, *Manners, Morals and Sex in America:* A History of Ideas (New York: Bookman Associates, 1953), pp. 371–72.

33. Henry R. Carey, "This Two-Headed Monster—the Family," *Harpers Magazine*, 156 (January 1928), 162–71.

34. Anonymous, "A case of Two Careers," *Harpers Magazine*, 158 (Janury 1929), 194–201.

35. Quoted in Lorine Pruette, "The Flapper," op. cit., p. 583.

36. Morton M. Hunt, *The Natural History of Love* (New York: Alfred A. Knopf, 1959), pp. 344–45

37. Neff, *We Sing Diana*, p. 201.

38. Judge Ben B. Lindsey and Wainwright Evans, *The Revolt of Modern Youth* (New York: Boni and Liveright, 1925), pp. 56–62.

39. Pruette, "The Flapper," op. cit. p. 581.

40. Samuel D. Schmalhausen, "The Sexual Revolution," *Sex in Civilization*, p. 416.

41. Alfred C. Kinsey, et al., *Sexual Behavior in the Human Female* (Phil.: W.B. Saunders Co., 1953), p. 298.

42. Christina Simmons, "Companionate Marriage and the Lesbian Threat," *Frontiers: A Journal of Women's Studies*, IV, 3 (Fall 1979), 54–59.

43. See, e.g., Marie Stopes, Married Love (London: A.C. Fified, 1918); Theodore H. van de Velde, Ideal Marriage (1926; rpt. New York: Covici Friede, 1930); Gilbert von Tassel Hamilton, *A Research in Marriage* (1929; rpt. New York: M.D. Lear Publishers, 1948); G.V. Hamilton and Kenneth Macgowan, "Physical Disabilities in Wives," in *Sex in Civilization;* Wilhelm Reich, *The function of the Orgasm* (1926; New York: Orgone Institute Press, 1942).

44. Floyd Dell quoting Dr. Constance Long and Dr. Eleanor Bertine. See note 29. See also Meagher, op cit.

45. There are several ninteenth century works which do suggest that a woman might fail to adjust to her marriage because of her lesbianism: e.g., Adolphe Belot, *Mademoiselle Giraud, My Wife* (1870) and August Strindberg, *A Madman's Diary* (1887), but none of these are by English or American authors. In the 1920s Edouard Bourdet's play *La Prisonnière*, which dealt with a woman's failure to adjust to marriage because of her lesbian experiences, was performed in the United States as *The Captive* and was a succès de scandale. See Jonathan Katz, *Gay American History: Lesbians and Gay Men in the U.S.A.* (New York: Thomas Crowell, 1976) pp. 82–91.

46. Katherine Bement Davis, *Factors in the Sex Life of Twenty-Two Hundred Women* (New York: Harper and Bros., 1929) pp. 247–48.

47. Ibid., p. 257.

48. Hamilton, *A Research in Marriage*, pp. 52–53.

49. Ibid., pp. 488–89 N.B.

50. Ibid., p. 497.
51. Ibid., p. 496.
52. Ibid., p. 495.
53. Davis, pp. 309–12.
54. A.C. Kinsey, W.B. Pomeroy, C.E. Martin, and P.E. Gebhard, *Sexual Behavior in the Human Female* (Philadelphia: W.B. Saunders, 1953).
55. Kinsey, pp. 452–53.
56. "Girl Love Test Gets Barbs," *Sacramento Bee,* May 15, 1973.

Strange Country This: Lesbianism and North American Indian Tribes

Judy Grahn
San Francisco

ABSTRACT. This article is an exploration of historical names and functions of gay and lesbian people among traditional North American Indian tribes. Some detailed descriptions of individual offices are included, such as "manly hearted" women and shamanic cross-dressing men, as well as the original definition of "dyke" and "ceremonial lesbian" as described by Paula Gunn Allen (Laguna Pueblo).

"Strange country, this," a white man wrote of the Crow Indians in 1850, "where males assume the dress and perform the duties of females, while women turn men and mate with their own sex."[1] Not only the Crow, but likely most Indian tribes on the American continent exhibited this same "strangeness." Sue-Ellen Jacobs studied written records from the last few centuries for references to homosexuals in American Indian tribes. Her figures reveal how prevalent Gay traditions were for the people who occupied this continent when the European colonial population arrived. Out of 99 tribes who kept written records, 88 made reference to homosexuality, with 20 including specific references to lesbianism. The latter references are more remarkable considering how little information has been re-

Ms. Grahn teaches gay and lesbian studies at New College of San Francisco and is the author of the book *Another Mother Tongue: Gay Words, Gay Worlds,* a work of gay cultural history. She received the *American Poetry Review's* award for Poem of the Year in 1979, and a Before Columbus Foundation American Book Award in 1982 for her book *The Queen of Wands.* Correspondence should be addressed to the author, 507 Liberty Street, El Cerrito, CA 94530.

This article is excerpted from *Another Mother Tongue: Gay Words, Gay Worlds* by Judy Grahn. Reprinted by permission of Beacon Press.

corded about anything concerning women, let alone information about lesbianism. The other 11 tribes denied any
homosexuality to the anthropologists and other writers. All
the denials of the presence of homosexuality came from
East Coast tribes located in the areas of heaviest and long-
est contact with those segments of white Christian culture
that severely punish people who admit to homosexuality.
The 88 tribes that reported homosexual culture include
many familiar Indian names: Apache, Navajo, Winnebago,
Cheyenne, Pima, Crow, Shoshoni, Paiute, Osage, Acoma,
Zuni, Sioux, Pawnee, Choctaw, Creek, Seminole, Illinois,
Mojave, Oglala, Shasta, Aleut, Fox, Iowa, Kansas, Yuma,
Aztec and Maya. Less familiar names include the Tlingit,
Naskapi, Ponca, Menomini, Maricopa, Klamath, Quinault,
Yuki, Chilula, and Kamai.[2]

Jacobs lists the exact offices held by homosexuals in 21
tribes, presenting a cross section of the functions, especially
those of cross-dressing people who took on the work, dress,
and social position of the opposite sex while establishing
sexual and even marital bonds with their own sex. Among
the Crow, for instance, cross-dressing homosexual men are
responsible for cutting down the tree that is used for the sun
dance ceremony. In 12 of the 21 tribes Jacob cites with
regard to homosexual functions, transvestites were the
medicine people or shamans of the tribe. In 4, the Crow,
Cheyenne, Dakota, and Illinois, they were essential for high
spiritual ceremonies; in 3 they served a special function at
funerals; in 1, the Winnebago, they acted as oracle; and in 1
tribe their role is reported as "good-for-nothing."[3]

In *Gay American History,* Jonathon Katz has collected
accounts mentioning the names Indians have used to des-
ignate their homosexual tribal members. Each tribe had,
or continues to have, special names for homosexuals, especially when referring to cross-dressing and special tribal
offices rather than to casual homosexual relations. The
Pomo use "Das," the Kalekau "Das" and "Murfidai" (for
hermaphrodite); the Mojave say "Alyha" and "Hwame"
(lesbian), while the Navajo call their homosexual priest-
hood "Nadle"; the Winnebago say "Siange" ("sigh-an-
gee"). The Oglala call homosexual magic men "Wintke,"
the Omaha and Ponca both say "Mingu-ga," the Zuni of

the Southwest say "Ko'thlama," the Yurok's word is "Wergern," and the Acoma Pueblo people say "Mujer-ado," a term believed to come from the Spanish "Mujer-hado," "man-witch-woman"; the Chippewa use "A-go-kwa," the Lakota "Adi-wa'lona" and "Koskalaka"; the Inuits say "Choupan," the Konyagas of Alaska say "Ach-nutschik." The Kamchadale of the Bering Strait call their homosexual magicians "Koe'kcuc", while the Kodiaks call theirs "Ke'yev." The Absaroke Indians of Montana use "Bo-te," meaning "not-man, not-woman," who among the Indians of the Santa Barbara region, were called "Jewel," which the Spanish recorded as "Joya." The transvestites of both sexes of the Klamath people are called "Twlinna ek," and when lesbians live together it is known as "Sawa linaa." Yuma Indians call lesbians "Kwe rhame," and homosexual men "Elxa"; female transves-tites are "War'hameh" for the Cocopa people and "Wa-rharmi" for the Kamia of California.[4]

WHAT'S IN A NAME

The European soldiers, trappers, explorers, and settlers were contemptuous of homosexual traditions in their own cultures, and several centuries of persecution under the In-quisition had taught them to deny all homosexuality. The heaviest persecution of homosexuals in Europe happened concurrently with the heaviest periods of colonization of the Indians in North America, according to Paula Gunn Allen. Small wonder, perhaps, that homosexuals were often the first Indians killed, and that even when tribes were tolerated by the white people, their homosexuals were mocked and perse-cuted to the point that the homosexuals changed their behav-ior for the sake of their people's safety. Balboa, for instance set wild dogs on the homosexual medicine men of California tribes, killing them, the "Jewels" of their own people.[5]

The white people coined a term for the homosexual Indi-ans they saw, the cross-dressers who lived among members of the opposite sex. They called them "Berdache," some-times translated "Bowdash" or "Bundosh." "Berdache" is a French word meaning "slave boy," probably stemming from the period when patriarchal Moroccan customs were brought to southern Europe by the invading Muslims.[6]

That the Indians themselves had extremely high opinions of their homosexual population is best illustrated by the offices homosexuals held within tribal life and by the openness with which they lived, even marrying members of their own sex in some tribes. A Kutenai woman of Montana, for instance, who dressed as a man and was accompanied in her travels by another woman the white writer described as the former's "wife," held the occupations of courier, guide, prophet, warrior, and peace mediator.[7]

Matilda Coxe Stevenson, an anthropologist, wrote about homosexual men in the Zuni tribe of the late 19th century, speaking of two cross-dressed men in particular as "being the finest potters and weavers in the tribe. One was the most intelligent person in the pueblo, especially versed in their ancient lore. He was conspicuous in ceremonials, always taking the part of the captive Kor'kokshi in the dramatization of the Ka'nakwe."[8] Stevenson also wrote a remarkable account of the death of her close friend, We'wha, a Zuni man who "passed" all his life as a woman and was prominent in the tribe. "Owing to her bright mind and excellent memory," Stevenson wrote, "she was called on . . . when a long prayer had to be repeated or a grace was to be offered over a feast. In fact, she was the chief personage on many occasions. On account of her physical strength all the household work requiring great exertion was left for her, and while she most willingly took the harder work from the others of the family, she would not permit idleness; all had to labor or receive an upbraiding from We'wha, and nothing was more dreaded than a scolding from her."[9] She once spent six months in Washington, D.C., visiting President Grover Cleveland and other politicians.

Overall, the collected accounts indicate the high status accorded Gay male transvestites who, usually at adolescence, took on the dress, language, gestures, and occupations of the women of the tribe. In part, this high status can be attributed to the high status occupied by Indian women in most tribes. For instance, the pottery making and weaving for which the Zuni homosexual man was noted are occupations constituting a major source of income for the Zuni people, and both are women's work. Land was and is usually held in trust by the women of a tribe, who also own the houses, hogans, teepees, yurts, and pueblos.

Paula Gunn Allen helps explain the woman-based philosophy prevalent in Indian tribalism, especially in Allen's own southwestern pueblos. You cannot understand the Indian way of thinking, she claims, without understanding that it stems from a spirit-based, rather than a family-based, system. "Among American Indians, spirit-related persons are perceived as more closely linked than blood-related persons. Understanding this primary difference between American Indian values and modern Euro-American Judeo-Christian values is critical to understanding Indian familial structures and the context in which lesbians functioned. For American Indian people, the primary value was relationship to the spirit world. All else was determined by the essential nature of this understanding. Spirits, gods and goddesses, metaphysical/occult forces, and the right means of relating to them, determined the tribe's every institution, custom, endeavor and pastime. This was not peculiar to inhabitants of the Western Hemisphere, it was at one time the primary value of all tribal people on earth."[10]

In the Indian belief system, human beings live in a universe that is, as Allen says, "alive, intelligent, and aware," and the spirits have as much to say about it as humans do. A number of spirit people belong to one's family, and one or more of them act as a person's personal guide. Put very simply, when (often in adolesence) through dreams, visions, or public rites, these spirits tell a person to put on the clothing, language, habits, and occupation of the opposite sex, the person does so. Not to follow the guidance given would mean a serious breach of the cultural value and a danger to one's self.

Modern patriarchal society has usually defined "natural" to mean rigid adherence to sexually dictated roles delineated by a body of authorities over what constitutes the masculine and the feminine spheres of society. The Indian idea of what is natural to a person means what the person's visions and spirits tell her or him to do. Some tribes have described homosexuality as something a being is born with;

others say it comes in a vision or is given to a person by a spirit. Others have special "tests" to find the boys who seek girls' tools and the girls who seek boys' tools. In the past, according to Jacobs, California tribes frequently used the method of seating a boy on the ground. "On one side of him are placed the tools or weapons representing manhood, on the other side some implements of woman's work. The grass is set afire around the boy. As he flees from the burning grass, he will grab something from one side or the other. His selection will be the factor determining his future."[11] In other tribes, such as the Aleut and Tabatulabal, parents might deliberately raise a boy to be a girl if he is particularly handsome.[12] Or else a shaman may choose the change for a boy or a girl.

Records indicate that having a homosexual nature and undertaking cross-dressing created a pool of initiates from which certain priesthoods of shamans drew their apprentices. Edward Carpenter reported that homosexuals among the tribes of the Bering Strait, the Kamchaldales, the Chukchi, the Aleuts, the Inuits, and the Kodiak Islanders, flourished under the direction and leadership of the shamans. A Chukchi lad of 16 who put on women's clothing, took up women's work, and moved a husband into his yurt was encouraged by the shamans, who took it to be an injunction of their own particular, and homosexual deity. Such youths, called "choupans," often went on to become priests, although not all of them met the requirements of character, temperament and calling.[13]

Entrance into the spirit world of shamanism was difficult and required tremendous effort, as writer Elie Reclus described:

> Disciplined by abstinence and prolonged vigils, by hardship and constraint, he must learn to endure pain stoically and to subdue his bodily desires, to make the body obey unmurmuringly the commands of the spirit. Others may be chatterers; he will be silent as becomes the prophet and the soothsayer. So the young novice becomes a solitary figure in the northern landscape, wandering through long winter nights across great plains with the white moon over him and the wind for

his companion. Absorbing the chill moonlight he feels himself in the presence of his greatest god, Sidne, the Eskimo mother goddess.

Like Demeter, Sidne visits the underworld, and so will he. Reclus continued:

> He sees stars unknown to the profane; he asks the secrets of destiny from Sirius, Algol and Altair; he passes through a series of initiations, knowing well that his spirit will not be loosed from the burden of dense matter and crass ignorance, until the moon has looked him in the face, and darted a certain ray into his eyes. At last his own Genius, evoked from the bottomless depths of existence, appears to him, having scaled the immensity of the heavens, and climbed across the abysses of the ocean. White, wan and solemn, the phantom will say to him: "Behold me, what dost thou desire?" Uniting himself with the Double from beyond the grave, the soul of the [apprentice] flies upon the wings of the wind, and quitting the body at will, sails swift and light through the universe. It is permitted to probe all hidden things, to seek the knowledge of all mysteries, in order that they may be revealed to those who have remained mortal with spirit unrefined.[14]

Girls of this region also undertook the homosexual crossover. Carpenter wrote that among the Eskimo people and other populations, especially in the Yukon, girls sometimes declined marriage and childbearing. "Changing their sex, so to speak, they live as boys, adopting masculine manners and customs, they hunt the stag, and in the chase shrink from no danger; in fishing from no fatigue. They are dykes, in other words, not alienated modern dykes, but dykes with a well-defined and respected social function."[15]

In "Transformations: Shamanism and Homosexuality," Mike Wilken points out that the Mojave Indians have, or once had, a special song cycle for the initiation of a sacred homosexual person, whose role was "highly elaborate and well integrated into Mojave cosmology."[16] An early re-

corder, George Devereux, said cross-dressers were excep-
tionally powerful shamans, especially the Huame, the
women. Homosexual Mojave shamans sometimes special-
ized in curing venereal diseases and were considered lucky
in love. They took marriage partners of their own sex.[17]

Formerly, the leadership among Navajos was reported by
Navajo informants to be the homosexual shaman/priest-
hood, the Nadle. Each family tried to have at least one of its
members affiliated with the Nadle, as such a sacred person
brought wealth and success to the whole family. As a group,
the Nadle were put in charge of the clan's wealth. Sources
quoted as late as the 1930s said that the Nadle were sacred
and holy and that without them the Navajo would perish as
a people. One speaker compared their leadership to that of
President Roosevelt. The word Nadle encompasses both
women and men.[18]

MANLY HEARTED WOMEN

Paula Gunn Allen states that among the Sioux were
women known as "manly hearted women."[19] They functioned as warriors and, at least sometimes, married other
women. "Among the Cherokee there were women known
as Beloved Women who were warriors, leaders, and influential council members. But among the Cherokee, all
women had real influence in tribal matters until reorga-
nization was necessitated by American removal attempts."[20]

According to Allen's research, Indian women spent most
of their time with each other, and men with men, as is
common among all tribal peoples. Sexual attitudes were
very free, and Allen feels it is likely that lesbianism was an
"integral part of Indian life." Simple sexual bonding with
accompanying warmth and friendship is only one aspect of
being homosexual, however, though it may be the most
prevalent as well as the easiest to hide. What of the cross-
dressing person, the lesbian warrior or chief, the shaman
who seeks and finds visions? "It might be," Allen says,
that:

> some Indian women could be seen as "dykes," while
> some could be seen as "Lesbians," if you think of

"dyke" as one who bonds with women in order to further some Spirit and supernatural directive, and "Lesbian" as a woman who is emotionally and physically intimate with other women. [The two groups would not have been mutually exclusive.]

The "dyke" (we might also call her a "ceremonial Lesbian") was likely to have been a medicine woman in a special sense. She probably was a participant in the Spirit (intelligence, force-field) of an Entity or Deity who was particularly close to earth during the Goddess period though that Deity is still present in the lives of some American Indian women who practice Her ceremonies and participate actively and knowingly in Her reality. Signs of this Deity remain scattered all over the continent: Snake Mound in Ohio is probably one such holdover. La Virgin de Guadalupe is another. There are all sorts of petroglyphs, edifices, and stories concerning some aspects of Her, and Her signs are preserved in much of the lore and literature in many tribes.[21]

In Allen's own Laguna tribe, the chief deities were female, and tribal relations were built around soroates, or sisterhoods. The Keres creator goddess, Thought Woman, created her two sisters by the power of Creative Thought, and together the three "gave rise to all creations."[22]

Given that in white Euro-American terminology a dyke is a woman who cross-dresses at least to some extent and is often found doing work, sports, games, and other activities that have formerly been the exclusive preserve of men, "manly hearted woman" is an Indian title that could translate as "dyke."

A detailed account of such a "ceremonial Lesbian," a Kutenai Indian in Montana in the early 1800s, appears in Katz's *Gay American History*. A member of a Plains tribe that valued hunting above everything else, she achieved a lively reputation as a courier, guide, prophet, warrior, peace mediator, and healer, as well as hunter. She changed her married name, Madame Boisverd, to one of her own language and choosing, Kauxuma Nupika, "gone to the spirits," after returning to her tribe after a year's absence. She said that while living among the whites she had magically changed her sex. Thereafter, she only wore men's clothing, gambled, warred, and "took wives" just as the men did, traveling with them over the countryside. Just how "wifely" some of her lovers were, however, is indicated in this record kept by frontiersman Alexander Ross: "In the account of our voyage I have been silent as to the two strangers who cast up at Astoria, and accompanied us from thence; but have noticed already, that instead of being man and wife, as they at first gave us to understand, they were in fact both women—and bold, adventurous amazons they were."[23]

Having lived a shaman's life, "Gone to the spirits," who also called herself Sitting-in-the-water-Grizzly, was given a shaman/warrior's death; that is, she was nearly impossible to kill. Set upon in a Blackfoot ambush, she did not falter until a number of shots had entered her body, and when several warriors slashed her with knives on the chest and abdomen the cuts were said to have healed themselves. Finally, one of the warriors opened her chest and cut off the lower portion of her heart. Only then did she die. The Indian informant who passed on the story, ended it by saying, "No wild animals or birds disturbed her body which is said to have gradually decayed."[24]

This woman was an example of a female homosexual, female shaman, a "ceremonial dyke," to borrow a phrase from Allen's analysis, which illustrates that the initiate was "required to follow the lead of Spirits and to carry out the task they assign her." Such stories, Allen says, are frequent in the literature and lore of American Indians. Such a crisis in the life of the initiate resulted in her "death" or deathlike trance, and then

> her visit to the Spirit realms from which she finally returns, transformed and powerful. After such events, she no longer belongs to her tribe or family, but the Spirit teacher who instructed her.

> The Lakota have a word for some of these women, koskalaka, which is translated as "young man," and "woman who doesn't want to marry." I would guess that its proper translation is "lesbian" or, colloquially, "dyke." These women are said to be the daughters

(that is, the followers/practitioners) of wila numpa or Doublewoman. (Pronounced Weeya-Noompa). Doublewoman is a Spirit/Divinity who links two women together making them one in Her power. They do a dance in which a rope is twined between them and coiled to form a "rope baby." The exact purpose or result of this dance is not mentioned, but its significance is clear. In a culture that values children and women because they bear them, two women who don't want to marry [a man] become united by the power of wila numpa and their union is validated by the creation of a rope baby. That is, the rope baby signifies the potency of their union in terms that are comprehensible to their society, which therefore legitimizes it.[25]

That the ceremonial or shamanic lesbian of tribal times often perceived virginity as a necessary part of her office is evident in this description of a female warrior in Carolyn Neithammer's book *Daughters of Earth:* Among the Kaska, in Canada, lesbianism was not only accepted but actually initiated and encouraged at times. If a family found itself with too many daughters, one of the girls was selected to be a son and was raised like a boy. When the child was five, her parents tied the dried ovaries of a bear to her inner belt. She wore them for the rest of her life as an amulet to prevent conception. Dressed in male clothing and performing the male role, these persons became outstanding hunters. Their sexual experiences were with other women, and orgasm was achieved by clitoral friction while one woman lay on top of another. If a male ever made advances to such a man-woman, he risked having his bow and arrows broken by the object of his attentions, for any sexual contact with a man was believed to ruin a lesbian's luck with game.[26]

A similar understanding that sexual relations with the opposite sex will ruin a shaman's power is expressed by Maria Sabina, a poet-shaman of contemporary times who practices healing, divining, and envisioning among her people, the Mazatec Indians of Mexico. Sacred hallucinogenic mushrooms help her with her craft. She describes herself in her chants as a spirit woman who can speak with the dead "be-

cause I can go in and out of the realm of death."[27] She has
been married more than once, and during those periods she
does not eat the mushrooms or practice shamanism because,
as she says, "the woman who takes the mushrooms should
not have relations with men."[28] "When one goes to bed with
a man their cleanliness is spoiled. If a man takes them (the
mushrooms) two or three days after he uses a woman, his
testicles rot. If a woman does the same, she goes crazy."[29]

WHITE CULTURE SUPPRESSED INDIAN HOMOSEXUAL TRADITIONS

The influence of anti-homosexual elements in white culture has altered the social position of homosexual Indians
within their tribes during the centuries of white colonization. This had correlated with a similar loss of power by
Indian *women* within the tribes. Numerous writers have
commented on the change in attitude toward homosexual
medicine people. In 1940, A. L. Kroeber wrote, "While
the institution was in full bloom, the Caucasian attitude
was one of repugnance and condemnation. This attitude
quickly became communicated to the Indians, and made
subsequent personality inquiry difficult, the later berdaches
[homosexuals] leading repressed or disguised lives."[30] Arthur Evans went so far as to suggest that the repulsion for
homosexual behavior felt by the whites caused them to use
harsh and genocidal methods against the tribes, annihilat-
ing many of them.[31] Most contemporary scholars believe
the purpose of such brutal attacks was to acquire the land
and resources of the Indians, and of course this did hap-
pen. But that is only the physical side of the story. I believe that the suppression of the often woman-centered and
pagan tribal life was a powerful underlying motive.

By 1889, shame already was attached to the homosexual
role among the Winnebago people, who had formerly highly
honored and respected homosexual persons. But the tribe
"had become ashamed of the custom because the white
people thought it was amusing or evil."[32] Another writer
noted that a Chippewa homosexual man was "scorned, in-
sulted and greatly belittled by the American travelers who

met him." White writers referred to sodomy as a "beastly and loathsome sin." Navajo men seldom dress as women now because they fear the ridicule of white people. Those who persist are considered queer and are referred to jokingly by white and Indian society alike, and children are discouraged in cross-sex affiliations.[33] As Allen has pointed out, much of the anti-homosexual sentiment among modern American Indians can be attributed to their attempts to secure a "safer" position among the dominant whites, as well as to their contact with Euro-American anti-homosexual forces in school, religious training, the army, and other institutions.

Along with the increasing repression of homosexual culture among modern Indian tribes trying to survive in a sea of Euro-American pressures, American Indian women have suffered and continue to suffer abuse and loss of their traditional powers. Homosexual culture goes hand in hand with a strong woman-based society, and such a society was at the very heart of the Indian culture that has been most under attack by white philosophy and practice. Homosexual people from tribes, villages, groups, and clans all over the earth are presently experiencing, or historically have already experienced, the suppression and loss of publicly acknowledged "office" that American Indian homosexual priests and medicine/shaman people have experienced over the last three centuries.

NOTES

1. Edwin T. Denig, "Biography of Woman Chief," in *Gay American History*, ed. Jonathon Katz, New York: Crowell, 1976, p. 308. The story is of a Crow woman of great powers who became a hunting chief and married four wives. She did not cross-dress.

2. Sue-Ellen Jacobs, "Berdache: A Brief Review of the Literature," *Colorado Anthropologist* 1 (1968); 25–40. Jacobs lists all eighty-eight tribes. Thanks to Mary Redick for bringing the article to my attention. See also Carolyn Neithammer, "Lesbianism," in *Daughters of the Earth* New York: Collier, 1977. Evelyn Blackwood, "Sexuality and Gender in Certain Native American Tribes: The Case of Cross-Gender Females," unpublished paper, has described cross-gender lives and the full acceptance of Lesbian marriage among five American Indian small-game hunting tribes along the Colorado River: the Mojave, Klamath, Maricopa, Yuma, and Cocopa. Among people who lived in small kinship bands and had egalitarian social structures, girls who rejected women's work as children would be accepted as men (among the Mojave this

included an initiation ceremony), and they married women who were not cross-gendered. They had Lesbian sexual relations; the woman might take a man for her next husband, or the two females live together a long time, raising the woman's children. In Western Gay terminology, they are butch and femme. According to Blackwood, these free Lesbian practices have become suppressed since the mid-1800s as tribes have needed approval from the white world and as men's economic status in the world has been accorded more importance, leading them to see cross-gendered Lesbians as competition for the labor of women.

3. Jacobs, "Berdache," p. 35.

4. Jacobs, "Berdache"; I also drew names from "Native Americans/Gay Americans: 1528–1976," in Katz, *Gay American History*, pp. 281–332.

5. Katz, *Gay American History*, p. 289. See also Arthur Evans, *Witchcraft and the Gay Counterculture* (Boston: Fag Rag Books, 1978), for other accounts of the suppression of Gay Indians.

6. *Random House Dictionary of the English Language*, unabridged (New York: Random House, 1966). *Berdache:* from French *bardache*, Spanish *bardajo*, Arabic *bardaj*, "slave." The sense is of "kept boy prostitute." Many people, especially earlier white writers, have used the term *berdache* (usually pronounced ber-dachie) when discussing Gay Indian customs. As far as I know, the Gay customs of traditional American Indian people had nothing to do with keeping boy prostitutes, and I have preferred to avoid the European term *berdache* when possible, using instead more original tribal words and names even when I cannot determine the exact meanings. When I do not have the original Indian name, I have used *Gay* or *dyke*, or *fairy* because these European words have ceremonial, tribal, and shamanic derivations and origins. They stem from underlying European Gay tribal cultural functions, rather than implying their suppression, as I believe, "Arab slave boy" does.

Currently, an intertribal network of modern Indian Lesbians are calling themselves "berdache" or "berdache women." I assume this is to distinguish themselves from white Lesbianism and to make certain they are known and identified as Indian women with a separate American history of their own, while using a term that does not spring from tribe in particular, as each tribe is quite different from another.

7. Katz, *Gay American History*, p. 293.

8. Katz, *Gay American History*, p. 314.

9. Katz, *Gay American History*, pp. 315–317.

10. Paula Gunn Allen, "Beloved Women: Lesbians in American Indian Cultures," *Conditions* 7 (1981): p. 70.

11. Jacobs, "Berdache," p. 29.

12. Jacobs, "Berdache," p. 28.

13. Edward Carpenter, *Intermediate Types Among Primitive Folk: A Study in Social Evolution* (London: George Allen & Company, 1914), p. 18.

14. Carpenter, *Intermediate Types*, p. 19, quoting Elie Reclus.

15. Carpenter, *Intermediate Types*, p. 18.

16. Mike Wilken, "Transformations: Shamanism and Homosexuality," unpublished paper.

17. Katz, *Gay American History*, p. 305.

18. Evans, *Witchcraft*, p. 102.

19. Allen, "Beloved Women," p. 67.

20. Allen, "Beloved Women," p. 67.

21. Allen, "Beloved Women," p. 81.

22. Allen "Beloved Women," p. 81.

23. Katz, *Gay American History*, pp. 293–298.

24. Katz, *Gay American History*, p. 298, quoting Francis Simon.

25. Allen, "Beloved Women," p. 82.

26. Neithammer, "Lesbianism," pp. 230–231.

27. Alvaro Estrada, *Maria Sabina: Her Life and Chants,* trans. Henry Munn (Santa Barbara: Ross-Erikson, 1981), p. 65.

28. Estrada, *Maria Sabina,* p. 44.

29. Estrada, *Maria Sabina,* p. 67.

30. Cited in Jacobs, "Berdache," p. 209.

31. Evans, *Witchcraft,* chapters 7, 8, 9.

32. Jacobs, "Berdache," p. 30, quoting Dorsey.

33. Jacobs, "Berdache," p. 30.

The Lesbian Corporate Experience

Marny Hall, PhD
San Francisco, California

ABSTRACT. By means of semi-structured interviews, this study investigates the work experience of 13 lesbians employed by large corporations. The respondents, who were already discredited for being women, had to manage the further potentially discrediting information of their lesbianism. The author examines the strategies used to manage such information. Because these strategies frequently included deception, the respondents then had to design a series of counter-strategies to avoid seeing themselves as dishonest. Each woman's strategy was unique; nevertheless, certain perceptions and approaches were common to all the respondents.

During the last 40 years, women's participation in the labor force has increased dramatically. In 1940, approximately a quarter of all American women were working outside the home; by 1975, the proportion had risen to almost 50% (Mackinnon, 1980) and has continued to increase. Currently, 65% of all women between the ages of 25 and 34 work (Horn & Horn, 1982). One sub-population of women, lesbians, are particularly well represented among the ranks of employed women.

LESBIAN FOCUS ON WORK

Most lesbians work. Out of the the 962 who responded to questionnaires sent out by Jay and Young, (1977), 671 (70%) had an occupation or a profession. Three-quarters of the other 30% were students, presumably preparing for a career. The data from Blumstein's and Schwartz's (1983) survey is comparable: 85% of the 1,554 lesbian respon-

---

Dr. Hall is a psychotherapist in private practice, and is the author of the book *The Lavender Couch: A Consumer's Guide to Psychotherapy for Lesbians and Gay Men.* Correspondence and reprint requests may be addressed to the author, 4112, 24th Street, San Francisco, CA 94114.

59

dents were either partially or fully employed. Only 1%
were strictly homemakers. In her study, Moses (1978)
found that 82 (90%) of the 92 lesbians who responded to
her questionnaire were working. Only 2 (8%) of the 24
lesbians interviewed by Tanner (1978) were not employed
full-time.

Such marked career focus may be related to the unfeasi-
bility, for lesbians, of other options. Unable to marry le-
gally, lesbians are not entitled to share their partner's as-
sets. Women earn significantly less than men and are less
able to support someone else. In addition, the egalitarian
values of the women's movement do not encourage the
subordinate-dominant role dichotomy implied by unequal
financial arrangements (Tanner, 1978). The infrequent assumption of traditional heterosexual roles by lesbians is
substantiated by survey data gathered by Brooks: out of
675 lesbians only 29 (4%) reported being supported by a
mate (Brooks, 1981). A final reason for lesbian focus on
work may have its roots in homophobia. Ranking high as a
goal with lesbians is career success or professional achievement, according to Brooks. Lesbians want to work. It may
be one area which can compensate for the failure ascribed
by the dominant culture to a lesbian lifestyle.

PREVIOUS RESEARCH

Lesbian work experience has not been as extensively explored as lesbian experience historically (Katz, 1976; Faderman, 1980) or the steps toward a lesbian identity (Cruikshank, 1981; Stanley, 1980). Aside from brief mention by
Lewis (1979), Ponse (1978), and Baetz (1980), demographic surveys of lesbian populations have been the primary source of information about lesbians in the workplace
(Jay & Young, 1977; Bell & Weinberg, 1978; Blumstein &
Schwartz, 1983). In these surveys, questions about work
are usually limited to two areas: the effect of being lesbian
on one's career, and whether respondents have "come
out" at work. In their pilot study of 289 women, Bell and
Weinberg (1978, p. 361) found that 21 (7%) had had negative experiences because of being lesbian. Nearly two-

thirds of the 361 respondents in Brook's (1980) study could not be sure that they would not lose their jobs if their lesbianism were known.

In 1980, The National Gay Task Force (NGTF) distributed a questionnaire which focussed exclusively on the experience of lesbians and gay men at work; 386 of the 1,500 questionnaires distributed were completed. Of that number, 235 (61%) thought their homosexuality would be a problem at work, if it were known, while 124 (32%) said they would not have the same job security as a heterosexual. An even 100 (26%) said it was unlikely they would be treated as an equal by heterosexuals, and 89 respondents (23%) said that they might lose customers or clients. Out of 386 respondents, 81 (21%) replied that they had actually experienced discrimination because of their homosexuality (National Gay Task Force, 1981).

The same NGTF survey was distributed at a meeting of career-oriented lesbians in San Francisco in 1980. There, the survey revealed that 38 (78%) of the 51 women responding to the questionnaire felt their lesbianism, if disclosed, would be a problem; 22 (45%) thought they would not have the same job security; 18 (38%) thought they were unlikely to be treated as equals; and, 25 (54%) thought they would lose customers or clients (Hall, 1981).

When lesbians feel that coming out would be harmful, they are likely to stay closeted. Of the 289 lesbians interviewed by Bell and Weinberg (1978), 115 (45%) had not told a single co-worker they were gay. In the study by Moses (1978), 72 (88%) concealed their lesbianism at work. Hall (1981) found that only 10 (20%) of the 51 members of the lesbian career-oriented group were completely open at work.

Though most respondents saw their lesbianism as detrimental in their work settings, there were some exceptions: 4% of the 289 lesbians polled by Bell and Weinberg (1978) said it had had a positive effect on their careers, and several felt their homosexuality especially qualified them for their particular work. It is worth noting that black lesbians in the Bell and Weinberg study were more likely to find their sexual orientation helpful than were white lesbians. A possible explanation is suggested by a black male respondent's comments in Hall's (1981) study. He felt his gayness was a benefit: "It's an advantage to me, like being black. The underground has helped me assimilate into the company."

Russo (1981) interviewed 55 gay men and lesbians who were leaders in the gay lesbian movement. All, it turned out, were self-employed or owned their own businesses, all considered themselves completely open about their gayness/lesbianism, and 35 of them (64%) said they were successful because they were gay.

One can speculate that one's work environment, and the sexual orientation of a boss, clients, and colleagues affect the work experience of a lesbian or gay man. Independent, openly gay professionals are likely to have gay/lesbian clients and colleagues who serve as a buffer against the homophobia which is part of most non-gay settings.

THE STUDY

Large corporations have never been particularly congenial settings for workers who have diverged from the norms of white, heterosexual, male society. A lesbian who works in such a setting has to face two levels of devaluation: her femaleness and her lesbianism. If she is not white and Anglo Saxon, she adds a third. Kanter (1977) describes the plight of the token woman in the corporation. Because she is different, she is thrust into the spotlight and her performance is constantly scrutinized. She has to work against a stereotype. The simple tasks she sets out to perform take on symbolic meanings. As Kanter points out, "She does not have to work hard to have her presence noticed, but she does have to work hard to have her achievement noticed" (p. 216). Such pressure increases the probability that the other layer, the discreditable lesbianism, will slip out inadvertently and add to the devaluation the lesbian is already experiencing as a female.

The problems of concealing a potentially discreditable identity are compounded in the corporate setting by the role the modern corporation often plays in the lives of its employees. As extended family, spa, health center, the corporation has taken over functions previously assumed by relatives, neighborhoods, and communities. The line between work and leisure is blurred.

Included in the new roles the company plays is that of matchmaker. A number of articles in the last few years describe the evolution of this new function. (Neugarten & Shafritz, 1980; Horn & Horn, 1982). Horn and Horn write, "We . . . find replacement families at our jobs. We socialize with co-workers, confide in them, trust them with our problems, and share our joys with them. So it's natural that men and women turn to the office to find prospective mates." (p. 3,4).

Lesbians in corporations stand out not only for being women, but also for not fitting into the new corporate culture which extends far beyond bounds of 9 to 5.

METHOD

Through friends, and by attending meetings of lesbian business and professional organizations, I met a number of lesbians working in corporations. I lunched with several of them individually, and met with a group of lesbian and gay employees who worked for the same corporation. From these discussions, I devised the interview questions, which reflect the themes and issues brought up by the women. The questions were open-ended and designed to evoke the ways in which the respondent experienced her lesbianism at work.

PARTICIPANTS

To find respondents, I continued the networking process. I contacted friends of friends and put notices in the newsletters and on the bulletin boards of gay/lesbian business organizations. Through this procedure I obtained 13 lesbian respondents. The interviews, which lasted between 40 and 70 minutes each, were held in offices, during lunch in restaurants, or in respondents' homes. I structured the sessions loosely to allow respondents to diverge from the questions and talk about whatever was relevant to them.

Of the 13 interviews, 10 were taped. During the non-taped interviews, I either took notes or reconstructed them from my memory immediately afterward. In the case of the 10 taped interviews, I took notes and transcribed them directly when I listened to the tapes after the interviews.

PROCEDURE

Because I am a lesbian I had to have a method of analysis that acknowledged the inter-subjectivity between the inter-viewer and the interviewee. Phenomenology was the method I chose because it includes the observer in the phenomena observed and emphasizes non-measurable aspects of pheno-mena, "the layer of living experience through which other people and other things are first given to us." (Merleau-Ponty, 1962, p. 57).

Following Giorgi's procedure (1975), I arrived at a de-scriptive statement of the experience. My steps were to: (1) use research-subject dialogues as the method for collecting data; (2) analyze each person's data for common themes; (3) look at the themes in relation to the experience; and, (4) integrate the themes into a descriptive statement of the experience.

RESPONDENTS

Of the 13 women interviewed, 4 (31%) held lower or middle management positions; 4 (31%) worked in techni-cal jobs; 3 (23%) had clerical jobs; 1 (8%) was in sales, and 1 (8%) was in personnel. All worked in corporations employing more than 100 people. Everyone interviewed fell between the ages of 27 and 40, except for 1 woman (8%) who was 22. Within the group, 2 respondents (16%) had been at their companies for 10 years, 1 had been at her job for 7 years (8%), and the remaining 11 (84%) had been at their companies from 1 1/2 to 4 years.

RESULTS

Experiences constantly occurred in the work setting that triggered the women's awareness of their lesbianism. Anti-gay jokes, or comments presuming heterosexuality, such as "Why don't you get married? . . . you're almost 28," stimulated an awareness of being different. Because being lesbian was not a socially desirable attribute, these women were constantly preoccupied with concealing that aspect of their lives. Sometimes concealment occurred as automatically as retinal adjustment to light change. At other times, it was deliberate and felt more stressful. Whether automatic or deliberate, the process of concealment called for constant attention to every nuance of social interaction. The background buzz of assumptions became centrally important for the lesbian because it signaled where vigilance was necessary or where she could relax and "be herself." The work reality for the lesbian, therefore, was one of a heightened awareness, a sensitivity toward the usually hidden matrices of behavior, values, and attitudes in self and others. The basic fabric of focused consciousness, what was important and what was not, was altered.

The respondents knew of the danger of disclosure in several ways. If they had not experienced discrimination directly by losing a job or missing a promotion, all had experienced it in the homophobic attitudes of co-workers. After Harvey Milk, the gay San Francisco city supervisor, was assassinated along with Mayor George Moscone in 1978, one woman's boss said, "Good . . . things needed to be cleaned up." Another woman, not known to be homosexual, was warned by a well-meaning co-worker to stay away from another co-worker who wore a "dyke" pin. Other respondents experienced direct discrimination against lesbians and gays. One woman knew two lesbians who were fired for being open at work, while another respondent lost a coveted project because the supervisor was told she was lesbian and he refused to work with her. Another woman, who had lived with her lover for 7 years, had earned enough sales points for a company sponsored trip to Hawaii; however, she had to go alone.

Accompanying the need for protective secrecy was a

"state-of-siege" mentality, a feeling of "us and them." Often the feeling associated with these states was anxiety or anger, or both, sometimes in the form of intellectual distance: "I don't fit in, and I don't necessarily want to"; "They're so ignorant"; "You just have to see where they're coming from."

Even if a subject's lesbianism continued to be a well-kept secret, it was perceived as a disadvantage, as "unfair treatment." No matter how long they had lived with their partners, they couldn't tap into corporate benefits, such as "family" health insurance. If they were relocated there were no family allowances. Nor could they play the management game because they would never have the requisite opposite-sexed spouse and a country club membership in the suburbs.

Being secretive meant both inner conflicts, "I wanted to come out, but I just couldn't," and constant anxiety about discovery: "If my bosses knew, they'd find a way to get rid of me"; "In the case of my supervisees, sometimes it gets emotional, and they might hug me. What would go through their minds if they knew I was a lesbian?"

Several women felt that their lesbianism, because it was invisible, would hold them back less than their gender, which they could not disguise. Being a woman was a major disadvantage in the corporate world: "As a woman, I'm generally assumed to be incompetent whereas the men are assumed to be competent unless proven otherwise."

Their lesbianism reinforced the separation between work and leisure. Some respondents contended that this was congruent with their needs: "I am a private person anyway. Even if I weren't gay, I wouldn't want to mix work with my life outside work." For others the discontinuity was a source of frustration and anger: "For these guys, they go home and their friends are the same people they see all day. For me, coming to work is bowing out of my world completely and going into theirs."

The respondents felt conflict between the need or expectation to be normally open and friendly and their realization that if they were they would not be perceived as "ordinary." If one is a lesbian and shares the ordinary events of one's day-to-day life, one shows that one is different from everyone else. If one conceals or distorts, then one is perceived as being like everyone else. One way to avoid this paradox was simply to avoid heterosexual co-workers. Several respondents said they tried to keep out of personal situations: "I maintain a professional air and shy away from those issues. I never socialize with them." Another common strategy to cope with this paradox was to dissociate oneself from part of one's behavior. In the same interview, respondents would talk about ways of concealing their lesbianism while stating firmly, "I don't hide my gayness." By dissociating from their actions, they kept secret from themselves and avoided the anxiety that would have been caused.

Several comments indicated that at times the respondents experienced their lesbianism as a source of strength. "Because I am gay, I have more confidence." And "There's a feeling of camaraderie."

At times, being misapprehended enhanced their status. Because one woman's partner was invisible to management, she was presumed to be unmarried and mobile, and was therefore offered special training in another city. Another woman in a non-traditional job felt that because she was seen as masculine, she was given more challenging job assignments than some of her counterparts who were seen as feminine.

Most respondents felt that disclosing their lesbianism would be damaging; thus, concealing their homosexuality became crucial, although frequently they felt concealing it was out of their control. For example, one woman was showing a friend from work the plans of the new house she and her lover had bought. Pointing out the master bedroom on the floor plan, she accidentally said, "This is where we sleep." She was appalled to have revealed the intimate nature of her relationship. Other respondents felt they revealed their lesbianism through their physical appearance. A lesbian who wore jeans to a clerical job said, "The way I dress I was in a way forcing it down their throats." Another woman said, "At the time they started suspecting, I made a mistake and cut my hair short. That was the tip-off."

There were many stories present within the study group

of one's homosexuality being revealed inadvertently. In one instance, a woman was featured in the business section of her hometown newspaper when she became the 300th member to join a local gay business organization. She had not been out at work before the article appeared. Another woman said her co-workers knew about her when her lover, wearing jeans and short hair, stopped by her office one day to drop something off. These accidental disclosures generated embarrassment and fear and were perceived by respondents as an "Oh, no!" experience. Even when the consequences were not as bad as feared, they were remembered vividly.

Those respondents who had a choice about disclosure still felt uneasy about it. Certain experiences compelled them to be open and balance the feelings that disclosure would be harmful. Friendship with a co-worker was the primary impetus: "We'd gotten very close and she shared a lot about her personal life. She kept talking about some gay friends of hers who tended to keep to themselves and exclude her . . . how disappointed she felt. I thought she was trying to let me know it was o.k. to come out." Another impetus for disclosure was feeling misunderstood, depersonalized, or victimized. One woman said, "They sit there every day and make cracks about gays. I don't say anything. One day I'm just going to yell 'Surprise. I'm one of them.' "

Even if respondents wanted to come out on such occasions, they usually didn't. Instead, they suppressed or translated the impulse into an act that revealed anger, but not their lesbianism. After listening to several co-workers complain about the recent political appointment of an open lesbian, "Isn't it terrible . . . all the fruits running around," the respondent went to a nearby storeroom and started sorting and heaving boxes. "I hadn't said what I wanted to," she said, "but at least we had the cleanest storeroom in the company by the end of the afternoon." Some respondents made an art of transforming their feelings in such hostile situations taking pride in how well the act went. When one woman heard anti-gay comments, she simply asked if the person being discussed did a good job. "That usually shut them up," she said. She said the same thing when people commented about blacks or other devalued groups. Thus, she managed to defend gays without seeming like a gay rights advocate, a reputation which she felt would have been injurious. Instead, she appeared liberal. Suppression or transformation took many forms. Lesbians didn't respond to comments, changed the subject, misrepresented themselves, brought "dates" to office functions, and even had separate house-warming parties—one for heterosexual co-workers and one for lesbian friends.

For some respondents, concealment of their homosexuality was automatic and caused no discomfort. Others felt uncomfortable and some were extremely distressed at what they saw as self-betrayal. One woman said, "I'd just come back from a gay rights march . . . and yet in that situation with those people I knew I'd be working with, I couldn't say anything . . . It was extremely upsetting."

At certain times, respondents chose to reveal their lesbianism. Such disclosures had both the qualities of premeditation and impulsiveness. Describing this, one respondent said, "I'd thought about it for a long time, but I didn't know when or if I was going to tell her . . . Then one night we had a few drinks and it just came out." Usually the respondent carefully chose the person to whom she was disclosing herself. Often, the disclosure and the reaction were anticlimatic: "I don't know how she felt . . . She didn't say much." Or "He said when I told him, 'I knew it . . . I just wondered if you cared enough to tell me.' " Or "Nobody seems to think it's as important as I do."

Disclosure had the paradoxical effect of magnifying the problem of concealment because now one or more others were included. After they felt an initial release, their tension was increased because of the greater possibility of inadvertent disclosure. The new heterosexual confidante didn't have the same investment in secrecy as did the lesbian involved and had nothing to lose and perhaps something to gain by passing on the woman's secret. And respondents had the additional worry of implicating their friends. If their lesbianism became known widely, their lovers or friends who worked in the same company might also be labeled as lesbians.

One woman saw revealing her lesbianism as a part of her

growth process, feeling it her mission to educate people.
Rather than sharing a secret, she intended to widen hori-
zons. She said, "I like to come out in a way that's natural . . . in an undercurrent way that doesn't call attention
to me . . . [It] just reinforces that we are everywhere . . .
Like the gay riots where people are talking about 'those
gays' I just said, 'yes, it's true that we don't have to express
our anger that way.' "

When respondents came out to co-workers whom they
suspected were homosexual, the exchange was more of a
ritual. Respondents would "have a sixth sense" about
someone else's orientation and begin to drop hints about
gay bars, restaurants, or cultural events that would be
meaningful only to other gays and lesbians. Such remarks
would often make an actual announcement unnecessary.

Conversely, some respondents made a point of staying
away from co-workers who seemed too openly gay. One
woman, describing the unwanted attention of another lesbian in the same company, said:

> She had masculine traits . . . the way she walked . . .
> the way she talked . . . and she was very open about be-
> ing gay . . . and she talked about her female lover . . . I
> got to know her . . . I don't remember how . . . but it
> got to the point where she came to visit me in my of-
> fice . . . and I was very uncomfortable . . . because of
> her image. I guess the first couple of times she came to
> visit, I visited. Finally I just explained that I was very
> busy.

Concealment did not necessarily stop in the case of respondents who were known to be lesbian. To maintain a
low profile, many of the women avoided conversations that
would highlight their lesbianism. One respondent said,
"Even if it would be appropriate to add something about
my lover because of the turn in the conversation, I don't
because I don't feel comfortable derailing the conversations. I don't want to be a curiosity." Another respondent
said, "Everyone knew we were lovers. We didn't dance
together even though other people were. I just didn't want
to cause any social discomfort."

All respondents felt variations in their work patterns. Some variations were attributed to differences in work load, others to mood and morale, and others to external personal events. No one attributed variations in work pace to homosexuality. Yet most respondents felt their future options were limited by their lesbianism. They could advance to a certain level but not beyond because they could not project the necessary corporate image. Some seemed not to care; several said, "I'm not ambitious"; some were resigned: "I've definitely settled for less." Others aimed for careers other than business where their lesbianism wouldn't be an obstacle, several planned to go into business for themselves or to become freelance consultants, and others took refuge in technical areas in which they had little interaction with co-workers.

In response to one question about how they would like to change their organizations or their own behavior, most respondents wanted to reenact what they had suppressed because of their fear of disclosure. "I'd like to stand up a little tougher than I did." But most respondents felt hopeless about changing their organizations. The task seemed overwhelming. When the hypothetical situation of working in a mostly gay company was posed, most respondents were surprised at their answers. They would aspire to higher jobs, expect to be more successful, feel more relaxed, more "like themselves."

DISCUSSION AND CONCLUSIONS

Karr (1978), McConaghy (1967), and Morin (1975) have established experimentally the presence of adverse feelings toward individuals assumed to be homosexual. Additionally, in Karr's experiment, individuals who labeled others as homosexual were frequently regarded positively by observers. Given such a strongly charged atmosphere, we can expect women who define themselves as lesbian in this culture to have developed strategies to maneuver in inimical environments. The corporate workplace is a potentially hostile environment. It reflects the values of the dominant white heterosexual male culture. Any deviation from this

norm, if not compensated for by extraordinary achievement or Affirmative Action laws, results in everything
from less status, less opportunity, and loss of co-workers'
esteem, to ostracism, harassment, and firing.

A group tends to develop its own strategies. Women, for
example, have "felt constrained to begin in areas of spe-
cialization for which they could claim special insight or
ability." (Warner, 1962, p. 227), or they have sought men-
tors (McLance, 1980). According to Cheek (1976), a black
strategy has been to "shine 'em on . . . don't let the white
man know what you really feel and think." (p. 16). Similarly, from the analysis of the interviews, it can be con-
cluded that lesbian employees have developed strategies
for dealing specifically with homophobia in the corporation. Some strategies cause disharmony and have to be
compensated for by others that restore balance. Some
strategies seem to be a permanent part of the disguise;
others are stepping stones toward self-disclosure which, in
itself, may simply be another strategy for dealing with
stigma. As Goffman (1963) notes, "There may be no 'authentic' solution at all." (p. 124).

Testifying to the the stigma felt by lesbians is the extent
to which they use non-disclosure as a strategy. The intense
observation of details which escape others is part of the
non-disclosure strategy. Bateson (1972) writes that we are
surrounded by an infinitude of detail and possible observa-
tions. The differences between a floor tile and a ceiling
tile, or two people's hair styles, do not necessarily constitute information. Information, according to Bateson, is
". . . a difference which makes a difference." (p. 453)

For most heterosexuals, subtle cues are not as important
as they are for the lesbian who feels herself to be in an
inimical environment in which a person's wedding ring,
interest in a professional football team, or use of personal
pronouns constitute a real difference. From these bits of
information, the lesbian can construct a hypothesis which
will guide her behavior. One can speculate that the stan-
dardization of clothing and tastes in the gay world is a
balancing strategy which compensates for the acute feeling
of being different at work. One needs the predictability of
gay ghettos to relax and luxuriate in trust and sameness.

All the forms of non-disclosure, whether the occasional substitute of "he" for "she" when describing a weekend outing with a lover or the complete fabrication of a heterosexual life, leave a lesbian in a morally untenable position. Not only is she lying, with all the opprobrium that a lie carries in our culture, but she is also ignoring the strong exhortations of the lesbian community to come out. In the foreword to *Out Of The Closets,* Jay and Young (1972) state that their book is written "in the hope that one day *all* gay people will be out of the closet." (p. 2).

BALANCING STRATEGIES

Denial and Dissociation: Frequently respondents would insist they were not in the closet, and in response to further questioning would contradict themselves, e.g., "No I haven't actually told anyone I'm gay." They continued to deny, however, that they were being secretive. Others claimed they felt comfortable in the face of homophobic remarks. Though no respondent said it, I speculate that these respondents were using a dissociative strategy; it was not *they* who were being discussed contemptuously. One respondent distinguished between "screamers" and "dykey women," and gays who "handled their gayness discretely." The dichotomization between good and bad gays is another dissociative strategy.

Avoidance: Several respondents simply avoided personal situations. Some regretted the absence of social interactions with co-workers. Others said they did not want to get close to co-workers because they had nothing in common with them.

Distraction: Respondents purposefully cultivated images which conveyed differentness—a feminist, a liberal—in order to distract from the more discreditable identification of lesbian.

Token Disclosure: While concealing the true nature of their relationships, some respondents would let it be known that they had done something with "a roommate." This was a partial disclosure since their roommates were also their lovers. Similarly, after Harvey Milk's assassination, one woman asked a homophobic job supervisor for time off to go to the funeral of a friend. She did not mention that the "friend" was Milk. In response to an anti-gay joke, one lesbian said, "You'd better get yourself some new material."

The most common partial-disclosure strategy was simply to disclose their homosexuality only to certain people they felt they could trust. Because this information could leak, such a partial disclosure often set off a new round of strategies to find out if one's secret had been more widely revealed. Whichever was used, all of these strategies seemed to restore respondents' threatened sense of integrity.

SUMMARY

The experience of being lesbian in the corporate world involves dynamics such as the past experiences of the lesbian employee, her current perceptions and future expectations, and the ways in which she is most willing and able to handle discontinuities within herself and between herself and the larger culture. "Coming out" is not an end point in the strategy of adjustment. Rather, it is a conceptual short cut, an abbreviated way of thinking which fails to encompass the extremely complex process of managing discrediting information about oneself.

REFERENCES

Baetz, R. (1980). *Lesbian crossroads*. New York: William Morrow.
Bateson, G. (1972). *Steps to an ecology of mind*. New York: Ballantine.
Bell, A. P., & Weinberg, M. S. (1978). *Homosexualities: A Study of diversity among men and women*. New York: Simon & Schuster.
Blumstein, P. W., & Schwartz, P. (1983). *American couples*. New York: William Morrow.
Brooks, V. R. (1981). *Minority stress and lesbian women*. Lexington, KY: D. C. Heath.
Cheek, D. (1976). *Assertive black . . . puzzled white*. San Luis Obispo, CA: Impact Publishers.
Cruikshank, M. (1981). *The lesbian path*. Tallahassee, FL: Naiad Press.
Faderman, L. (1980). *Lesbian-Feminism in turn-of-the-century Germany*. Tallahassee, FL: Naiad Press.
Giorgi, A. (1975). *Duquesne studies in phenomenological psychology* (Vol. 2). Atlantic Highlands, NJ: Humanities Press.

Goffman, E. (1963). *Stigma.* Englewood Cliffs, NJ: Prentice-Hall.

Hall, M. (1981). Gays in corporations: The invisible minority. Unpublished PhD dissertation, Union Graduate School, San Francisco.

Horn, P. D., & Horn, J. C. (1982). *Sex in the office.* Reading, MA: Addison-Wesley.

Jay, K., & Young, A. (1972). *Out of the closets.* New York: Links.

Jay, K., & Yuong, A. (1977). *The gay report.* New York: Summit.

Kanter, R. M. (1977). *Men and women of the corporation.* New York: Basic Books.

Karr, R. (1978). Homosexual labeling and the male role. *Journal of Social Issues,* 34(3), 73–83.

Katz, J. (1976). *Gay American history: Lesbians and gay men in the U.S.A.* New York: Thomas Y. Cromwell.

Lewis, S. (1979). *Sunday's women, a report of lesbian life today.* Boston: Beacon Press.

MacKinnon, C. A. (1980). Women's Work. In D. A. Neugarten & J. M. Shafritz (Eds.), *Sexuality in organizations* (pp. 59–66). Oak Park, IL: Moore Publishing.

McConaghy, N. (1967). Penile volume change to moving pictures of male and female nudes in heterosexual and homosexual males. *Behavior, Research, and Therapy,* 5, 43–48.

McLane, H. (1980). *Selecting, developing, and retaining women executives.* New York: Van Nostrand.

Merleau-Ponty, M. (1962). *Phenomenology of perception.* Atlantic Highlands: Humanities Press.

Morin, S. F. (1975, September). *Attitudes toward homosexuality and social distance.* Paper presented at the meeting of the American Psychological Association, Chicago.

Moses, A. E. (1978). *Identity management in lesbian women.* New York: Praeger.

National Gay Task Force. (1981). *Employment discrimination in New York City: A survey of gay men and women.* New York: Author.

Neugarten, D. A., & Shafritz, J. M. (1980). *Sexuality in organizations: Romantic and coercive behaviors at work.* Oak Park, IL: Moore Publishing.

Ponse, B. (1978). *Identities in the lesbian world: The social construction of self.* Chicago: Greenwood Press.

Russo, A. (1981, August). *Finding the gay elite.* Paper presented to the Association of Lesbian and Gay Psychologists at the meeting of the American Psychological Association, Los Angeles.

Stanley, J., & Wolfe, S. J. (1980). *The coming out stories.* Watertown: Persephone Press.

Tanner, D. M. (1978). *The lesbian couple.* Lexington, KY: Lexington Books.

Warner, W. (1962, October). Women executives in the federal government. *Public Personnel Review,* pp. 227–234.

To Write "Like a Woman": Transformations of Identity in the Work of Willa Cather

Joanna Russ

University of Washington

ABSTRACT. Willa Cather's early life resembles one of the histories in Jonathan Katz's *Gay American History*. Her cross-dressing,
invention of a male pseudonym, and details of behavior, together
with her love for two women in her adulthood, Isabelle McClung
and Edith Lewis, make it clear that Cather was a lesbian.

Defensive about *One of Ours*, Cather nonetheless wrote much
of her fiction in a male persona—*A Lost Lady, The Professor's
House*, "Tom Outland's Story," *Death Comes to the Archbishop,
O Pioneers!, My Ántonia*, and *One of Ours*, as well as numerous
short stories. Much of the fictional material in these works is
curiously inconsistent with the male persona, but instead resembles lesbian experiences: the inaccessibility (to the narrator)
of women who are nonetheless accessible to other men, absolute
heartbreak at the untouchability of the women rather than anger
or guilt or the search for sexual release elsewhere, and the
women's intimacy with the men involved, as in *One of Ours* or *O
Pioneers!*, without any suggestion of sexual involvement or explicit sexual history. Lesbian isolation, in adolescence at any rate,
produces such situations; Carson McCullers's and some of May
Sarton's work are cases in point.

Speaking in masquerade, Cather is capable of describing lesbian experience with a fullness and unconsciousness which is now
impossible. Innocence gave way to guilty self-consciousness, and
that to politically conscious rebellion. The gain is in honesty, but
Cather's record of lesbian experience, under whatever disguise, is
nonetheless irreplaceable.

How is a lesbian to write? Or to put the question more
accurately, how can a lesbian novelist use her experiences
and feelings, especially her sexual ones, in an era which
doesn't permit her to be open about them?

Joanna Russ is a professor in the English Department at the University of
Washington, Seattle, WA 98195. She won the Nebula Award in 1972 for her
short story "When It Changed," and the Hugo Award in 1983 for her novel
Souls. Reprint requests may be sent to the author at the above address.

Although Willa Cather's biographer, James Woodress, does not state openly that his subject was homosexual, her early life, as he describes it, very much resembled the lives of Alice Mitchell and Alberta Lucille Hart, who appear in Jonathan Katz's *Gay American History*.[1] By the age of 15, Cather had cut her hair "shorter than most boys" and was signing her name "William Cather, Jr." She had always played male roles in amateur theatricals, and even in college was "trying her best not to be a girl." She also still signed herself "William Cather," had a "masculine" voice, and made her entire elementary Greek class laugh when she first appeared in the college classroom because she looked like a boy from the waist up but was skirted from the waist down.[2] In adult life she was "obsessed with the desire for privacy"[3]—not surprising for a woman who "had no need for heterosexual relationships" (Woodress goes this far only to add "She was married to her art"), whose romances were with other women, and who called the death of one of her intimates, Isabelle McClung, "a thunderbolt." After McClung's death, according to Woodress, Cather hardly knew how to go on living, was in a comatose state, and was unable to feel anything. She also declared that all her novels had been written to Isabelle McClung.[4]

Even Cather's literary mentor, Sarah Orne Jewett, criticized her for adopting a man's point of view in her fiction, calling it a masquerade.[5] Woodress himself complains about Cather's "masquerades," as does the critic Mary Ellmann.[6] According to Woodress, Cather also received a great deal of criticism on the publication of her novel *One of Ours,* a novel in which the central consciousness is that of a young man, Claude Wheeler, and in 1921 she told a reviewer, in Woodress's words, that she "always felt it presumptuous and silly for a woman to write about a male character."[7] However emphatic such a declaration was, I believe it to have been placatory and very likely insincere, since the "presumption" was one the novelist insisted upon in most of her work, including the novels *A Lost Lady, The Professor's House,* "Tom Outland's Story" (a self-contained part of *The Professor's House*), *Death Comes to the Archbishop, O! Pioneers, My Ántonia,* and *One of Ours,* and short stories such as "Coming, Aphrodite," Paul's Case,"

"A Wagner Matinee," "A Death in the Desert," and the marvelous "The Enchanted Bluff." If Willa Cather was masquerading, it was a masquerade she returned to again and again, despite Jewett's advice, despite reviewers' possible reactions, and despite her own belief, spoken if not felt, that such a masquerade was silly and presumptuous. What had been common, respectable behavior between women during most of Sarah Orne Jewett's lifetime—"romantic friendship," "the development of affection between friends to the point where it becomes indistinguishable from love," women's love poems written to women, and "a model 'Boston marriage' [to Annie Fields] which lasted for almost 3 decades"[8]—such was by Cather's time simply perversion. Lillian Faderman traces this change of social climate in the last 2 decades of the 19th century. Krafft-Ebings's *Psychopathia Sexualis,*[9] first published in 1882, when Willa Cather was 9 years old, was the first widely influential text to establish the idea of female "inversion" as both morbid and a medical entity, and by the time Cather was in her early 20's any intellectual who had missed *Psychopathia Sexualis* in translation could find the same ideas in Havelock Ellis's also very influential *Studies in the Psychology of Sex* (1897).[10] The innocent rightness in feelings of love for and attraction to women which Jewett and her contemporaries enjoyed was not possible to Cather's generation; the social invention of the morbid, unhealthy, criminal lesbian had intervened. Indeed, when Annie Fields wanted to bring out a volume of Jewett's letters after Jewett's death, Mark DeWolfe Howe, Fields's friend and biographer, suggested that she omit four-fifths of the indications of the women's affection for each other lest readers misinterpret it.[11] This event is very reminiscent of the recent publication of Eleanor Roosevelt's letters to Lorena Hickok, after which the excuse/complaint the executor of the estate offered was that what seems to be so clear in the letters of course isn't, that readers just don't understand Roosevelt's effusive, old-fashioned style.[12] In view of the changed social climate in the early 20th century (American popular concern with lesbianism's morbidity began in the 1920s, but any au courant intellectual must have known about such matters much earlier), Willa Cather's "masquerade" was a necessity. Following Jewett's advice, specifically about an early story, "On the Gull's Road," and changing her heroes to heroines (Jewett wrote "a woman could love her—in the same protecting way—a woman could even care enough to—take her away from such a life"[13]) would have meant personal and professional disaster.

Cather's novels show distinct traces of this masquerade. In an earlier version of this paper I wrote that Cather's novels depict a world in which heterosexual relationships are impossible, but this is not really the case. Such relationships can appear in her work if they are described from a distance; they are impossible only to those of Cather's heroes who are at the center of the story's consciousness. And described over and over again is that these loves are not so much frustrating, enraging, or embittering as they are simply hopeless.

One of the things James Woodress chooses to find ridiculous in *One of Ours* is Claude Wheeler's wedding night, when his wife, Enid, literally locks him out of their train compartment, breaking Claude's heart. What is missing, says Woodress, is sexual frustration.[14] This is true. But there's more missing than that. What's missing is a whole complex of feelings which a real young man would feel under those circumstances, both in our day and in the era in which the novel occurs.

From literature, consciousness-raising groups, and psychotherapy groups, and from what men have told me, I have surmised what such a man would feel. First of all, he might not feel sexually frustrated in that particular scene for Claude, after all, is a virgin and can easily be thought of as rather frightened. But as the situation evolves, Cather makes it clear that Enid remains distant and disgusted, however physically available she may be, Claude would most certainly feel first of all angry, and the anger would be born of a feeling of entitlement. After all, he might well think, what did she get married for? What did she think marriage was about? A sensitive man, Claude would also feel the guilt that exists on the other side of the entitlement, that he was a cad for forcing himself on Enid, that he is bestial, that, given the era in which the novel is set, women really are more pure than men, and so on. What Cather creates instead is a kind of absolute heartbreak at the sheer untouchability of the woman and her rejection of Claude. In fact, one gets a very strong impression from the book that Enid might as well lock her bedroom door at night. They're married people living in the same house, and yet there's absolutely no sense of physical contact between them, not even in the negative forms of anger, bitterness, or frustration.

Even in *O! Pioneers,* where there is a tangible obstacle between the young couple—the young woman, Marie, is married to someone else—there are elements that simply do not make sense. Again, I doubt that a male writer would imagine the situation as Cather does, nor would a real man live it the same way. For one thing, Emil is not only in love with Marie, but remains so, monogamously and hopelessly, for several years, not even thinking of another woman during that entire time. (He certainly doesn't go and visit the local whorehouse, as he might very likely do in, say, a Hemingway story.) Again, it's not the specific physical frustration that's emphasized, but the emotional deprivation, the impossibility and hopelessness of the situation. Moreover, although she makes it clear that she will not become his lover, the woman responds with a great deal of affection. The two young people are surprisingly intimate, in an unchaperoned way, which strikes me as extraordinary for that time and place, although it would certainly not be strange for such a friendship to develop between two young women, a relationship in which one of them could feel at once extremely affectionate while also totally secure from any sexual problems or sexual advances.

In *The Professor's House,* no tangible obstacle separates the couple since the professor and his wife have been married for some years, and yet they clearly have not really spoken with or touched each other in a long time. There is no open anger, only resolute detachment on his side and chilliness on hers. In this novel occurs the absolutely astonishing imagery that Ellen Moers points out in *Literary Women:* the dress dummies in the professor's study, intensely seductive and soft to the eye, yet which when touched astonish and repel by the extremely unpleasant hardness of their texture.[15] (One might note here that the professor's study is a converted sewing room in the attic of the family house and that Cather's own study, in which she wrote *O! Pioneers,* was a converted sewing room in the attic of the McClung family house). Moers, in her passages on Cather's work, is very coy about naming the "ancient very female view of the nature of love" expressed by Cather, but there is no doubt that the love in question is lesbian, as the other writers she discusses in this connection make clear, including Woolf, Stein, and Colette. Nor is Tom Outland, who appears in the middle of *The Professor's House,* more sexual than the Professor, indeed, he is about as non-sexual a young man as one can find in literature—not unsexed, but in some strange way set apart from the possibility of any sexual act or occasion. The atmosphere of his stay on the mesa is so intensely, so transcendentally imaginative that the preserved female corpse found there, which he, his friend, and the priest who is his teacher call "Mother Eve," is a shock. Even more shocking is the priest's rather risqué hint that this ancient Indian woman may have been killed for adultery. The event, its unexpectedness and its surprising ugliness, parallels the shock of touching those seemingly generous and lovely dress dummies, only to find them extremely unpleasant.

The longer one looks at these stories, the less the feelings of the characters seem to match the novelistic situations. The Professor, although his detachment from his wife is matched by his detachment from life itself as expressed finally by his almost-suicide, has no specifically sexual memories of the past, just as Marie in *O! Pioneers* feels only sadness that she must remain married to a man she no longer loves. She's afraid of him, yet Cather gives us no memory or fearful anticipation of his making sexual demands of her. Again, what Cather emphasizes is the impossibility of the whole situation, well expressed by Emil's desire for one look of love from Marie's eyes and nothing more. The prohibition against adultery is not enough to explain a love that can be satisfied only in death. Rather, in one of the strongest scenes in the book, love is made identical with death; only in death can anything hap-

pen between the two women. In *The Professor's House,*
the Professor's "original nature" returns to him at middle
age after "his nature as modified by sex"[16] has somehow
disappeared. The misogyny he expresses throughout the
rest of the book results in an absolute lack of interest in
family life, his children, and "especially" his wife, whose
presence he cannot stand any longer and whom he describes as "chiselled . . . a stamp upon which he could not
be beaten out any longer . . . a hand holding flaming arrows," that is, something unbearable.[17]

Death, impossibility, monogamy, heartbreak, untouch-
ableness, loneliness, inevitable frustration—through these
Cather is making the very strong statement that the desire
for women, the love of women, is impossible to her protagonists. Other men may be entitled to it, as in Emil's
case in *O! Pioneers,* or achieve it, as in *A Lost Lady,* but
never is it accessible to the male character at the center of
the story. In *The Professor's House,* the Professor simply
gives it up. Never explicitly described in her fiction but
probably very real to Cather was the experience of living
outside a lesbian circle in an essentially heterosexual
world, where information about lesbianism did not exist,
where she was the only one of her kind (or thought she
was), and where the only women she could be attracted to
were heterosexual women who would respond with friendship, with a great deal of affection and concern, even perhaps with the considerable non-sexual touching permitted
between women, but with absolutely nothing more. In the
face of such total deprivation, the sense of specific genital
frustration Woodress complains of as missing in *One of
Ours* simply gets lost in the general starvation, and the
appropriate response becomes that of Claude Wheeler:
heartbreak, hopelessness, and helplessness.

If one goes back and translates the situations in Cather's
novels into lesbian situations, the fiction often makes
clearer sense. If Claude and Enid were women setting up
house together, one of them affectionate, the other passionate, then the horror of the affectionate one at the passionate one's passion and the consequent distance between
them make perfect sense, as do the passionate one's helplessness and hopelessness. The impossibility of Marie and

Emil's love and his extraordinary monogamy make sense. (Emil's showing off his Mexican costume to all the town girls in one scene in the book recalls young Cather's taking male roles in local dramatic productions. The costumes and roles are possible; the reality is not.) The bitterness of the young man who finds out that the heroine in *A Lost Lady* is having an adulterous love affair also makes more sense. The lady is available, all right, *but to men*. Moers calls the novel "an Electra story, raw and barbarous."[18]

Willa Cather grew up in an extremely deprived situation, one that did not end with the 19th century, a truth to which much contemporary writing by openly lesbian artists attests. Like most lesbian artists, she did not have the protection of (for example) Natalie Barney's money. Apparently she did not find an openly lesbian circle in which, for example, Renee Vivien could write openly of lesbian passion. She did not or could not risk her respectability. Such a situation is mitigated only somewhat by finding a partner; Jill Johnston has written very well of the "fearfully tenacious dependent isolated . . . declasse, illegal and paranoid marriage"[19] in which one clings desperately to the other precisely because there is no assurance that either of them will ever be able to find another partner, and even if one does, she will never be socially entitled to her. As Johnston convincingly shows, everyone and everything conspire to separate lesbian lovers, from the isolation forced on them by society to deliberate attempts by parents, friends, institutions, or merely heterosexual men who feel challenged, to break the couple up. In short, the sexual psychology depicted in so much of Cather's work is that of the lesbian in love with the heterosexual woman because she believes there is nobody else to be in love with. Lesbian writers who moved in a predominantly and openly lesbian society, like Radclyffe Hall or Djuna Barnes, did not seem to exhibit this psychology. (The misery of *The Well of Loneliness* was special pleading; Hall's *The Unlit Lamp* has no such deferring to prejudices.) I suspect many such writers face other phenomena such as Renee Vivien's guilt or the ghetto problem since their community, rejected by the larger society, is far too closed in; however, deprivation per se is not the same kind of problem. It is, however, a problem for writers who live, or have lived, in the same social context as Cather—for example, Carson McCullers. Again, in McCullers' work one finds the emphasis on imaginary rather than real satisfactions, and the presentation of mutual love as inherently impossible. And in May Sarton's *Mrs. Stevens Hears the Mermaids Singing,* there is something of the same feeling, that loving a woman is somehow transcendentally wonderful but always transitory, in some sense unspeakable if not actually impossible. The difference is always one of social context, of the possibility of honesty, and of the availability of sexual partners. Does this kind of ambiguous material in Cather make the work worse? I think not. If her male characters were in accord with either real male experiences or the literary traditions governing such things, we would merely have an addition (observed at second hand at that) to material which is in very long supply. Descriptions of female sexuality are rare, however, and rarer still are descriptions of lesbian sexuality. Nor does the "masquerade," the existence of lesbian feeling in Cather's work, seem to lessen the value of the work. Quite to the contrary, it was possible for Cather, in masquerade, to speak more completely, more clearly, and less self-consciously than could, for example, Djuna Barnes in *Nightwood.* The sense of alienation and the grotesque, which Bertha Harris finds admirable in lesbian literature,[20] is precisely what is missing in Cather. The male mask enabled her to remain "normal," American, public, and *also* lesbian. Even now, any openly lesbian writer is almost forced to be a self-conscious rebel, a position congenial to some, but one that can be constricting nonetheless; such a role Cather simply did not take or need.

I would suggest that, as an example, the character of Claude Wheeler is not one of Cather's greatest failures, as she and her biographer seem to think, but rather one of her greatest successes. The scene in which Claude imagines himself to be one of the world's "moon children" and his wife, Enid, to be one of the world's "sun children," is echoed in many fairly recent lesbian novels in which the protagonists feel themselves to be members of a world of darkness, not of the daily world of heterosexual social life. Yet how many of these characters have been able to do this kind of musing while lying on their backs under the moonlight on a Nebraska farm—and so un-self-consciously, so innocently, while so unaware of the presence of the moon in Western literature as a female symbol?

The innocence, of course, had to go. If the next stage can be called guilty self-consciousness, and the stage after that self-conscious rebellion, no matter what aesthetic advantages they offer (and I believe they offer many not available to Cather, honesty being one of them), they do not have the same advantages as Cather's masquerade; they cannot possibly create the aesthetic completeness and richness of Cather's work. Under whatever disguise, Tom Outland, Claude Wheeler, and so many of the other male personae of the books Cather gave us are, in a very precious and irreplaceable way, records not of male but of female experience, indeed of lesbian experience. In a sense not thought of by contemporary reviewers, and even possibly by Cather herself, Claude Wheeler and many other nominally male characters in Cather's work are, for lesbians, truly *One of Ours*.

NOTES

1. Katz, J. (1978). *Gay American history: Lesbians and gay men in the U.S.A.* New York: Avon Books. (pp. 390–414).

2. Woodress, J. E. (1970). *Willa Cather: Her life and art.* New York: Pegasus. (pp. 45, 53).

3. *Ibid.*, p. xi.

4. *Ibid.*, p. 173.

5. *Ibid.*, p. 132.

6. Ellmann, M. (1968). *Thinking about women.* New York: Harcourt, Brace & Jovanovich. Ellman speaks of Cather's "bluff, middy-blouse suspicions of . . . sexuality" (p. 114) and calls Claude Wheeler in *One of Ours* an aspirant to the feminine in spirit (p. 192). Ellman appears to be annoyed at Cather's attributing "male" virtues to her female characters, and "female" virtues to her male characters. I believe homophobia to have been at work here.

7. Woodress, p. 194.

8. Faderman, L. (1981). *Surpassing the love of men: Romantic friendship and love between women from the renaissance to the present.* New York: William Morrow. (pp. 197–199).

9. Kraft-Ebing, R. von.(1925). *Psychopathia sexualis.* (———, Trans.). New York: Surgeon's Book. (Original work published 1886.)

10. Ellis, H. (1911). Studies in the psychology of sex: Sexual inversion. Philadelphia: F. A. Davis. (Original work published 1897.)

11. Faderman, p. 197.

12. "Was Eleanor a lesbian?" *Seattle Gay News,* November 23, 1979.

13. Faderman, p. 202.

14. Woodress, p. 194.

15. Moers, W. (1977). *Literary women: The great writers.* Garden City, NJ: Anchor Books. (p. 359).

16. Cather, W. (1973). *The professor's house.* New York: Vintage. (p. 267).

17. *Ibid.*, p. 274.

18. Moers, p. 363.

19. Johnston, J. (1973). *Lesbian nation: The feminist solution.* New York: Simon & Schuster. (p. 157).

20. Harris, B. (1977, Fall). What we mean to say: Notes toward defining the nature of lesbian literature. *Heresies 3: Lesbian art and artists* (pp. 5–8).

My Gay Ántonia:
The Politics
of Willa Cather's Lesbianism

Timothy Dow Adams, PhD

West Virginia University

ABSTRACT. Although Willa Cather's lesbianism has recently been publicly acknowledged, her personal and artistic political decisions about the revelation of her sexual preference have not been explored. Most critics who acknowledge Cather's homosexuality see no traces in her fiction of what Lillian Faderman calls "same-sex love." Because of the political consequences of writing openly about lesbianism in the time that Cather came of age, according to Faderman, "perhaps she felt the need to be more reticent about love between women than even some of her patently heterosexual contemporaries because she bore a burden of guilt for what came to be labeled perversion." While it would certainly have been possible for Cather to live a discreet lesbian life without showing traces of her sexuality in her writing, it is more likely that her sexual preferences are present in her works, particularly in her most autobiographical book, *My Ántonia,* in the character who represents Cather, Jim Burden. The "emptiness where the strongest emotion might have been expected," the relationship between Antonia and Jim, is more understandable when we realize that both Jim Burden and Antonia Shimerda were imagined by Cather as homosexuals whose deep friendship was based on mutual understanding of their oddness in the heterosexual world of 1918.

After years of critical comment that avoided the issue of Willa Cather's homosexuality, or only hinted about it, in 1975 Jane Rule publicly identified Cather as a lesbian by devoting a chapter to her in *Lesbian Images,* although fail-

Timothy Dow Adams, Assistant Professor of English at West Virginia University, has published articles on autobiography, Austen, Melville, Hawthorne, Stein, Sukenick and others in such journals as *ESQ, Studies in the Novel, Clio, Critique, American Transcendental Quarterly,* and *Biography.* "My Gay Ántonia: The Politics of Lesbianism in Willa Cather" was presented at the 12th Annual 20th-Century Literature Conference at the University of Louisville, Louisville, KY. Correspondence can be addressed to the author, Department of English, West Virginia University, Morgantown, WV 26506.

ing to see any traces of lesbianism in Cather's fiction. Lillian Faderman, in *Surpassing the Love of Men,* her book-length study of love and romantic friendship between women, refers to Cather's forty-year relationship with Edith Lewis as a "Boston Marriage," a late nineteenth century term encompassing life-long friendship between women, with or without sexual relations. But like Rule, Faderman sees "absolutely no suggestion of same-sex love in Cather's fiction."[1] Because of the political consequences of writing openly about lesbianism in the time that Cather came of age, according to Faderman, "perhaps she felt the need to be more reticent about love between women than even some of her patently heterosexual contemporaries because she bore a burden of guilt for what came to be labeled perversion."[2]

While it would certainly have been possible for Cather to live a discreet lesbian life without showing any traces of homosexuality in her writing, it is more likely that her sexual preferences are present in her literature, whether consciously or unconsciously, and that an analysis of her work, particularly *My Ántonia,* in terms of homosexual images can add a new dimension to Elizabeth Sergeant's contention that "her books, provided one does not take them too literally, are a better guide to Willa Cather's life than any biographical dictionary."[3]

Sexual tension is never absent in Cather's books. As Blanche Gelfant notes in an article on sex in *My Ántonia:*

> Once we redefine his [Jim's] role, *My Ántonia* begins to resonate to new and rather shocking meanings which implicate us all. We may lose our chief affirmative novel, only to find one far more exciting—complex, subtle, aberrant.
>
> Jim Burden belongs to a remarkable gallery of characters for whom Cather consistently invalidates sex. Her priests, pioneers, and artists invest all energy elsewhere. Her idealistic young men die prematurely; her bachelors, children, and old folk remain "neutral" observers. Since she wrote within a prohibitive genteel tradition, this reluctance to portray sexuality is hardly surprising. What should intrigue us is the strange in-

voluted nature of her avoidance. She masks sexual ambivalence by certainty of manner, and displays sexual disturbance, even the macabre, with peculiar insouciance. Though the tenor of her writing is normality, normal sex stands barred from her fictional world. Her characters avoid sexual union with significant and sometimes bizarre ingenuity, or achieve it only in dreams. Alexandra Bergson, the heroine of *O! Pioneers,* finds in recurrent reveries the strong transporting arms of a lover; and Jim Burden in *My Ántonia* allows a half-nude woman to smother him with kisses only in unguarded moments of fantasy. Their dreams suggest the typical solipsism of Cather's heroes, who yield to a lover when they are most solitary, most inverted, encaptured by their own imaginations.[4]

Despite the use of such suggestive words as "aberrant," "involuted," "sexual disturbance," "macabre," "bizarre," and "inverted," in reference to Willa Cather's portrayal of sexuality in her characters in general, and particularly in Jim Burden, Blanche Gelfant sees these characters as merely afraid of sexual and emotional contact with each other, thus echoing Marcus Klein's thesis that "It is the struggle to get beyond the necessity of human relationships that is the secret history of all Willa Cather's novels."[5]

Although Jim and Antonia do transcend or avoid the necessity of expected human relationships—every reader has probably wondered why they did not marry when Jim returned to Black Hawk after Antonia had been deserted by Larry Donovan—the story, cast as it is in the form of a fictional combination of Jim's autobiography and Antonia's biography, is centered around the long-lasting and deep human relationship between the dual protagonists. And it is the confusing nature of that relationship that causes "emptiness where the strongest emotion might have been expected."[6] Jim Burden's autobiography focuses too much on Antonia to explain a normal friendship. A way out of these confusions lies in the realization that both Jim and Antonia were imagined by Willa Cather as homosexuals. Their attraction to each other is as deep as it is, not because they are

failed lovers, but because their friendship is reinforced by
the realization that their "aberrant," "inverted," sexual disturbance is basically homosexual. It is not surprising that
Willa Cather's lesbianism is reflected in both Jim and Antonia when we consider that Elizabeth Sergeant calls Jim "Antonia's twin-sister."[7] At one point Jim says to Antonia, "I'd
have liked to have you for a sweetheart, or a wife, or my
mother or my sister—anything that a woman can be to a
man."[8] One of the things that a woman can be to a man
when both are homosexuals is a confidante, a cover to shield
one's sexual preferences from others. As Frank Caprio
writes, "It is not uncommon for lesbians to establish friendly
relations with male homosexuals. One reason is that the
relationship is apt to be a platonic one and consequently
they have no need to fear being seduced, particularly if they
harbor antipathy toward men in general."[9] Homosexual
men and women are attracted to each other out of a common feeling of separation from societal norms and a common desire for non-sexual friendship, the kind of friendship
that exists between heterosexual men or women.

Although Antonia and Jim chose each other as play-
mates, they never seem to feel the slightest sexual interest
in each other, even in experimentation. At an age when
boys typically show their incipient affection for girls by
pulling their hair, chasing them, or affectionate indiffer-
ence, Jim and Antonia instead go for sleigh rides where
they "burrowed down in the straw and curled up close
together" (p. 52).

At first, Jim and Antonia seem to be acting out the standard male/female roles in the episode with the snake at the
prairie dog village: Antonia as the screaming, frightened
female, Jim as the calm, brave male. But in actuality the
situation is only, as Jim later realizes, "a mock adventure"
(p. 49), both in the sense that the snake is not really so
dangerous as it appears and in the mutual realization that
Jim and Antonia are only acting out their respective roles in
a pretense of normality. Although some critics see the
snake-killing episode as an authentic test of courage and
initiation into manhood,[10] it is clearly a false test, and both
Jim and Antonia realize that fact immediately. It is Antonia
who alertly spots the snake and her screams, unfortunately

delivered in Bohemian, are a warning rather than a cry of fright. Jim's reaction to the snake is hardly masculine: "His abominable muscularity, his loathsome, fluid motion somehow made me sick. He was as thick as my leg, and looked as if millstones couldn't crush the disgusting vitality out of him" (p. 45). Jim stands up to the snake only because he was too scared to think of running, while Antonia approaches the snake fearlessly, even though barefooted. The scene ends with Antonia calmly wiping Jim's sickened face. According to Blanche Gelfant's interpretation of this scene, which she feels has implicit sexual connotations, "as Jim accepts Antonia's praise, his tone becomes wry and ironic, communicating a unique awareness of the duplicity in which he is involved."[11] While Gelfant sees duplicity only in terms of the snake's oldness and the fact that the contest was "fixed by chance" (p. 50), Jim remembers the incident as a conscious agreement between Antonia and himself to mask their growing awareness of their sexual differences and "to confront deeply repressed images, to acknowledge for the only time the effect of "horrible unconscious memories."[12] "The ancient, eldest Evil" (p. 47) seen in the snake and in Jim's symbolic cutting of it, represents on one level another version of Adam and Eve's awareness of evil, and on another Jim's and Antonia's recognition of their latent homosexuality. Seeing his homosexuality as an ancient evil and remembering his first admission of it as a "horrible, unconscious memory," reflects Jim's sense, recalled years afterward, of the "guilt at the core" of homosexuality which "begins long before a sexual experience, with just the feeling of being different."[13]

As they mature, Jim and Antonia's sexual differences become more apparent. In Black Hawk, Jim shows little interest in Mr. Harling or in boys his own age, including Charley Harling, who live around him. Instead, Jim prefers the company of "Sally, the tomboy with short hair," (p. 149), who "always dressed like a boy" (p. 175), or the adult Frances, who replaces Charley in Mr. Harling's eyes as a son, father, and daughter walking "home together in the evening, talking about grain-cars and cattle, like two men" (p. 150). David Stouck sees that "The specific conflict that arises for Jim in Book III is sexual," and notes

that "the best times for Jim occur when men are absent—
when grandfather is at church and Mr. Harling is away on
business—leaving the carefree world of happy children
presided over by the indulgent Mrs. Harling, the older
daughter Frances, and Antonia."[14]

Antonia, meanwhile, has become even more masculine
in appearance and occupation. Calling herself Tony, as
Willa Cather called herself Willy, Antonia, whom Gelfant
refers to as an "ultimately strange bisexual,"[15] takes pride
in her maleness. With perspiration on her lip "like a little
moustache" (p. 130), Antonia says joyfully, "I like to be
like a man" (p. 138), while asking Jim "to feel the muscles
swell in her brown arm" (p. 138). While in town, Antonia
temporarily adopts a more feminine appearance, although
her voice is now "deep and a little husky" (p. 176). Although Antonia is presented in this section in more feminine terms, her basic lack of interest in the opposite sex is
still obvious. She does go happily to dances, but she is just
as glad to dance with the other girls, as she does in the
scene where she waltzes with Mary Dusak, knowing
"there's a roomful of lonesome men on the other side of
the partition" (p. 190). Some young men begin to notice
Antonia at the Vannis' tent dances, but Jim never mentions her being interested in any of them. Her love of
dancing is presented, not as romantic desire, but as a love
of physical activity common to the strong immigrant girls
whose "out-of-door work had given them a vigour" (p.
198) which is reflected in their dancing ability. Antonia
goes to the dances, not as a shy young farm girl, but by
breaking "into a run, like a boy" (p. 205). Although Antonia is popular with the town boys, the only sexual incident
with them involves Antonia slapping young Harry Paine
for kissing her.

Jim's lack of sexual interest in girls begins to cause questions about his masculinity: "Anna knew that whispers
were going about that I was a sly one. People said there
must be something queer about a boy who showed no interest in girls of his own age, but who could be lively
enough when he was with Tony and Lena or the three
Marys" (p. 216). To forestall these rumors, Jim attempts to
kiss Antonia in a sexual way. Antonia responds with sur-

prise and indignation. Having failed again at a heterosexual relationship, Jim bolsters his pride by imagining that he
"knew where the real women were, though [he] was only a
boy; and [he] would not be afraid of them, either" (p.
225). At this point in his remembrance of his sexual development, Jim recalls a pleasant recurring dream about Lina
Lingard in a short skirt, flushed and "carrying a curved
reaping-hook in her hand" (p. 225). The castration image
of the curved reaping-hook and cut wheat reinforces the
earlier image of the snake and the spade. Significantly,
even though he wants to, Jim is never able to have "this
flattering dream" (p. 226) about Antonia.

Later, Jim and Antonia are involved in what Stouck calls
"a sublimated erotic dalliance"[16] during a July picnic in the
country. Antonia and Jim's mock-erotic game is broken up
by the appearance of Lena, looking "almost as flushed as
she had been" (p. 238) in Jim's dream.

Although Antonia is banished from the Harlings to work
for the evil Wick Cutter because of her supposed sexual
encounters with boys, she actually dreads the thought of a
heterosexual experience. Cutter's sexual history and his
preparation to rape Antonia cause her to suggest that Jim
take her place, symbolically sleeping in her bed. Although
Cutter's attempted rape of Jim seems obvious, Jim's latent
homosexuality drives him deliberately to put himself in the
position of substituting for Antonia in a sexual encounter
with a man. Jim must have been aware of Cutter's plans to
seduce Antonia, yet he pretends to be asleep when he
hears Cutter's steps outside his room:

> The next thing I knew, I felt someone sit down on the
> edge of the bed. I was only half awake, but I decided
> that he might take the Cutter's silver, whoever he was.
> Perhaps if I did not move, he would find it and get out
> without troubling me. I held my breath and lay abso-
> lutely still. A hand closed softly on my shoulder, and
> at the same moment I felt something hairy and co-
> logne-scented brushing my face. (p. 248)

Jim's reaction to Cutter, who is earlier described as "a
peculiar combination of old-maidishness and licentious-

ness" (p. 211), is as excessive as his revulsion of the snake, and includes the same tone of disgust and sickness. "Vile as the Cutter incident is—and it's also highly farcical— Jim's nausea seems an overreaction, intensified by his shrill rhetoric and unmodulated tone."[17] Jim's awareness of his homosexual desires and his disgust at the nature of his encounter with another male combine to produce an out-raged tone of over-protestation that only emphasizes his sexual fears. As Clyde Fox notes, "I have never been rec-onciled to the feeling about the 'disgustedness' that Miss Cather gives Jim after he has been lewdly pawed over by Mr. Cutter. It would seem more natural to me for a boy to smother in a burst of anger whatever anti-homosexual emotions he might feel about it."[18]

Jim's homosexuality becomes more apparent by Book III. While at the University of Nebraska, he never dates or even talks to young women except for Lena Lingard, who reappears as in his dream still teasingly flirtatious. Al-though Jim and Lena frequently go to plays and dinners, their relationship is clearly asexual. Lena is at this point more nearly in Jim's social sphere; she seems to suggest a closer relationship, but Jim resists and they part with "a soft, slow renunciatory kiss" (p. 293). When the narrator of the introduction to *My Ántonia* describes Jim, she says that he still has "the romantic disposition which often made him seem very funny as a boy" (p. ii). This view of Jim as a funny boy is echoed by Lena who says to Jim just before they part—their "renunciatory kiss" sealing forever the chance of a sexual relation—that "You aren't sorry I came to see you that time? It seemed so natural. I used to think I'd like to be your first sweetheart. You were such a funny kid" (p. 293). Lena's statement, which seems similar to Jim's later remark to Antonia about having any relation-ship a man and woman can, supports the image of Jim Burden as a funny boy suggested by the narrator in the introduction. These repeated statements seem odd in light of the Jim Burden revealed in *My Ántonia,* one who never seems humorous. Perhaps the two people who see Jim as funny mean that he is funny in the sense of being odd in the role of a boy.

While Jim is at the university, Antonia deliberately enters a mock-heterosexual relationship with Larry Donovan, whose reputation as a scoundrel could hardly have escaped her notice. Her lesbianism being in conflict with her maternal instincts results in a deliberate attempt to live with Donovan so that she could become a mother without the worry that a traditional marriage would be expected. Even before she has her child, Antonia has returned to her mannish ways, wearing "a man's long overcoat and boots, and a man's felt hat with a wide brim" (p. 316). Jim and Antonia meet, and it is at this juncture in their lives that most critics feel they should have married each other.

Because Jim and Antonia understand each other's sexual preferences, they both feel the difficulty and sorrow of their individual attempts at solving the homosexual's dilemma in a heterosexual world. When Jim and Antonia meet again after 20 years, they have both solved that dilemma by contracting marriages of convenience that serve as masks for their sexual variance. Jim's wife is described by the narrator of the introduction, in the revised 1926 version, as "handsome, energetic, executive . . . unimpressionable and temperamentally incapable of enthusism . . . She has her own fortune and lives her own life. For some reason, she wishes to remain Mrs. James Burden" (p. ii). Jim's sterile, childless marriage is contrasted with Antonia's fruitful marriage to Anton Cuzak, but Antonia and Cuzak relate to each other more as friends than as lovers. As Alexandra Bergson says in *O! Pioneers,* "I think when friends marry they are safe."[19]

When Jim and Antonia are reunited at the book's end, they walk along the familiar roads of the divide. Thinking about their mutual homosexuality, Jim reflects that "For Antonia and for me, this had been the Road of Destiny; had taken us to those early accidents of fortune which predetermined for us all that we can ever be" (p. 372). The early accidents of fortune had caused each of them to leave the main road of heterosexual life for their personal destiny as homosexuals. For Jim and for Antonia, deep friendship based on mutual homosexuality was all they could ever share.

NOTES

1. Faderman, L. *Surpassing the love of men: Romantic friendship and love between women from the renaissance to the present,* (New York: Morrow, 1981), p. 21. For a discussion of historical and biographical evidence for Cather's lesbianism and her need to conceal her sexuality, see Sharon O'Brien's (1984) "The Thing Not Named": Willa Cather as a lesbian writer, *Signs, 9,* 576–599, which was published too late to be incorporated into this essay.

2. Faderman, p. 201

3. Cited in Slote, B., "Willa Cather," *Sixteen modern American authors,* ed. by Jackson Bryer (New York: Norton, 1973), p. 38.

4. Gelfant, B. "The forgotten reaping-hook: Sex in *My Ántonia,*" *American Literature, 43,* (1971), p. 61.

5. Klein, M., Introduction, *My mortal enemy* (New York: Vintage Books, 1926), p. 59.

6. Brown, E. K., & Edel, L. *Willa Cather: A critical biography,* (New York: Knopf, 1953), p. 202.

7. Cited by Lewis, E., *Willa Cather Living* (New York: Knopf, 1953), p. 149.

8. Cather, W., *My Ántonia,* (Boston: Houghton, Mifflin, Sentry Edition, 1946), p. 321. Further references are to this edition.

9. Caprio, F., *Female homosexuality,* (New York: Citadel Press, 1954), p. 87.

10. See for example Miller, J. E., "*My Ántonia:* A frontier drama of time," *American Quarterly, 9* (1958), p. 482.

11. Gelfant, p. 64.

12. Gelfant, p. 70.

13. Abbott, S., & Love, B., *Sappho was a right-on woman* (New York: Stein & Day, 1972), p. 20.

14. Stouck, D. *Willa Cather's imagination* (Lincoln: University of Nebraska Press, 1975), p. 51.

15. Gelfant, p. 73.

16. Stouck, p. 52.

17. Gelfant, p. 73.

18. Fox, C., "Revelation of character in five Cather novels," Dissertation. University of Colorado 1963, p. 211.

19. Cather, W., *O Pioneers!* (Boston: Houghton, Mifflin, Sentry Edition, 1913), p. 308.

Confronting Internalized Oppression in Sex Therapy with Lesbians

Laura S. Brown, PhD
Seattle, Washington

ABSTRACT. This paper focuses on a much-neglected aspect of therapy with lesbian clients: treatment of sexual dysfunction. It examines roots of dysfunction that can be found in cultural homophobia and misogyny, and presents a theoretical framework for intervention in the sexual problems of lesbian clients.

In the decade since the various psychotherapy professions have begun to recognize that homosexual relationships are a normative, although minority choice, rather than a deviation from a heterosexual norm, a number of questions have been raised regarding therapy with lesbian clients. In that decade, the therapy professions have done an about-face. Lesbian clients are now, more than ever, likely to receive support for their lives and choices rather than so-called therapy aimed at changing sexual and affectional preferences.

Although many aspects of work with lesbian clients have been addressed, the area of sex therapy has been badly neglected. The whole area of lesbian sexuality is shrouded in myth. One of the most pervasive of these myths is that "Women know intuitively what women want sexually," and that lesbians are thus less likely than heterosexual

Laura S. Brown received her PhD in Clinicical Psychology in 1977 from Southern Illinois University at Carbondale, with specializations in Psychology of Women and Human Sexuality. She is currently in private practice as a lesbian feminist therapist in Seattle, WA, where she also holds an appointment as Clinical Assistant Professor in the Department of Psychology at the University of Washington. She is a consulting editor of *Psychology of Women Quarterly,* chairs the Lesbian Issue Task Force of the Division of Psychology of Women of the American Psychology Association, and serves on the Steering Committee of the Feminist Therapy Institute. Reprint requests may be sent to the author, 4527 First, NE, Seattle, WA 98105.

women to be dissatisfied with their sexual functioning and seek sex therapy. Masters and Johnson, in fact, strengthened and gave scientific respectability of sorts to this myth when, in *Homosexuality in Perspective,* they attributed the sexual satisfaction of their homosexual experimental pairs to high degrees of intra-gender empathy (Masters & Johnson, 1978). The assumption seems to have been made by the few writers who touch on the subject that a lesbian, once having struggled through cultural homophobia to an acceptance of her sexual and affectional preference, will function well sexually past that point (Sisley & Harris, 1977).

Although no data exist on either the incidence or the prevalence of complaints of sexual dysfunction among the lesbian population, the clinical picture observed by this writer is that lesbians suffer from sexual dysfunctions of similar types and etiologies as do many heterosexual women. Lesbians are first and foremost women. Women's anti-social socialization in Western culture is a well-documented phenomenon (Barbach, 1976). Not surprisingly, the juxtaposition of two people with such socializations, as occurs in a lesbian relationship, carries with it some enhanced potential for problems in sexual functioning. In addition, factors related more specifically to the position of lesbians in a homophobic culture, and less specifically to actual genital sexual functioning, can also have an impact on sexual satisfaction for lesbians. It is the phenomenon that describes those factors, named herein as "internalized oppression," that will be addressed in this paper in connection to its relevance to the diagnosis and treatment of the sexual problems and complaints of lesbian clients.

Internalized oppression can be described as the process by which a member of an oppressed or stigmatized group internalizes into her or his core identity and self-concept all or part of the negative stereotypes and expectations held by the culture at large regarding that group. Internalized oppression is constantly reinforced and strengthened by real, external oppression. Internalized oppression can be manifested in beliefs and behaviors, either overtly and consciously or subtly and nonconsciously (Memmi, 1965).

For the majority of the lesbian clients who have sought me out for sex therapy, the conscious and overt manifestations of internalized oppression have long been discarded. Most of these women are articulate in expressing their pride in being both lesbian and female. Such clients are seeking, and may benefit most from, a positive and affirmative model of lesbian life. What has instead become increasingly apparent is that, in these women there is still a large amount of internalized, subtle, and nonconscious oppression manifested in ways which have direct as well as indirect effects upon sexual functioning and satisfaction.

Such subtle internalized oppression, which takes the form of both internalized misogyny and internalized homophobia, can be seen both in the sex histories of clients and in the nature of the presenting problems. One such marker of internalized homophobia common to the learning experiences of the majority of lesbian clients seen by this therapist has been the internalization of distorted images of lesbian sexuality gleaned from sources in the culture at large, such as pornography, psychiatry texts, encyclopedia entries on lesbianism, and popular novels. Clients report that the images they had observed regarding lesbian sexuality were bi-polar in nature. Either lesbian sexuality was portrayed as brutal, i.e., homosexual sexual assault taking place in prisons or back alleys, squalid, degrading, and drug-induced, i.e., both participants in a sexual act are in a state of consciousness altered by drugs or alcohol, and thus not responsible for their actions; or, conversely, lesbian sexuality was portrayed as wonderful, magical, exciting beyond words, and remarkable as a cure-all for female sexual ills, i.e., a previously preorgasmic woman is made love to by another woman and "cured" of her sexual dysfunction. The former model creates problems in the desire phase of sexual arousal (Kaplan, 1979). If a lesbian responds to this negative image of her sexuality, she may experience nausea, anxiety, and a sense of degradation and worthlessness in the presence of physiological signs of sexual arousal. Clients report self-medicating with alcohol, marijuana, and other depressant drugs in attempts to reduce anxiety when functioning sexually, phobicly avoiding sexual contact when sober, or both. Anecdotal evidence from gay and lesbian Alcoholics Anonymous groups suggests that re-establishment of sober sexual functioning is a major stumbling block in the recovery process. Upon achieving stable sobriety, many clients report for the first time in memory serious problems in experiencing sexual arousal.

The "lesbian-sex-is-magical" model, which appears positive and sexually harmless at first glance, can, when taken as a standard of performance to be sought after, become a source of self-criticism and performance anxiety and potentially lead to dysfunctions in either the arousal or orgasm phases of sexual activity. In such cases, I have encountered clients who enter therapy questioning their adequacy as lovers, women, and indeed as lesbians because they find themselves unable to measure up to standards set by the heroines of post-liberation lesbian romantic novels. These clients report experiencing "spectatoring," a process of critical and anxious self-observation that occurs during, and is inhibiting to, the arousal process, or find themselves comparing their own rate and intensity of arousal to that of their partners when one woman meets the idealized image and the other does not.

Both of these phenomena can be analyzed as having their psychological sources in homophobia, both external and internalized. In a cultural context where models of normative lesbian sexual functioning are lacking, the limited amount of information that is available to the average lesbian can become problematic for her in the development of her sexual identity. The woman who has learned from her reading, or from listening to the homophobic myths of family, clergy, or psychotherapists, that her commitment to, and enjoyment of, genital sexuality with other women is a signal of her taking the first step into a negative, marginal, and disparate lifestyle, may find herself terrified of her own sexual feelings. Conversely, the woman who feels that she must live up to some "Wonder-Dyke" image, in order to prove to herself and the internalized detractors in her head that those negative images are incorrect, is likely to experience considerable anxiety when her own frailties, limitations, and basic human qualities as a sexual partner become apparent. If in such a case the therapist is operating with a deficiency of information about the range and reality of normative lesbian sexual functioning, intervention itself can become part of the problem and lead to painful iatrogenic sexual problems for lesbian clients. Thus, whenever a therapist devises interventions in sex therapy with lesbian clients, she or he would be wise to seek out and be aware of the effects of internalized homophobia on the client's sexual self-concept, and then consciously avoid interventions that re-create the phenomenon in the course of therapy itself. In the context of taking a sexual history, this implies that the therapist engage in careful and highly specific questioning concerning the client's sources of early learning about lesbian sexuality. In addition, when working with a couple, the therapist must probe in order to ascertain what subtle messages either partner may have internalized regarding the loss of the right of lesbians to have a good-quality relationship in which both emotional and sexual intimacy are present. Evidence from my clinical practice, which has been corroborated by anecdotal information from both colleagues and acquaintances, suggests that many problems in sexual functioning experienced by lesbian couples serve as the "fly in the ointment," the problem in the relationship that satisfies the demands of a homophobic culture which believes that no relationship between two women can be entirely satisfying. The sexual problem functions as a self-fulfilling prophecy, strengthening the internalized stereotypes regarding the lower value of lesbian relationships and lending credibility to other internalized negative messages. In such cases, it is an important part of sex therapy, to work directly with these internalized negatives. From my experience, behavioral sex therapy of the sort described by Masters and Johnson has had little effect when clients have persisted in strongly-held, although often not overtly-expressed beliefs such as "This won't work anyway because all lesbian relationships are short and shallow," or "Lesbianism is just another closet for celibacy, so why work on being sexual." It is astonishing how frequently and regularly these and similar sentiments occur in client and non-client populations of lesbians, including self-identified feminist lesbians.

It is important to note here that the internalization of the "negative/degrading" stereotype of lesbian sexuality creates a dysfunction that is, in essence, a disorder of sexual desire. However, I have found it necessary to clarify, both for myself and for my clients, that a fear of lesbian sexuality is not synonymous with a general phobia of sexual desire; rather, such a fear more often functions as a survival mechanism developed in response to a genuine fear of the often very real negative consequences of responding to arousal in the context of a homosexual relationship. It behooves a therapist in such a situation to address the reality of the client's fears, which may encompass job loss, ostracism by her family of origin, or loss of access to her children, and both to validate their real nature while simultaneously allowing the client to develop alternatives for coping with these very real consequences of oppression, alternatives that will allow her to go beyond self-limiting anxiety in sexual situations.

Beyond the immediate impact of internalized oppression on sexual functioning is the unfortunate secondary effect that such oppression has inhibited the growth of woman-centered and lesbian-positive erotic imagery. Since many sex therapy techniques include the use of either commercial or educational erotica, it is problematic, although not surprising, that many lesbian clients find such male-created images either degrading or uninteresting. Therapists must be selective when suggesting erotic materials to clients and be sensitive to the anti-woman themes that are prevalent in most commercial pornography. I have found that supporting clients in the development of their own erotic images, stories, and stimuli has been a valuable pathway for clients who are attempting to reclaim their right to joyful sexual functioning. In addition, there is a growing body of erotic materials—written, drawn, and photographed—that is being created by lesbians for lesbians (Califia, 1980; Corinne, 1982, Nelly & Cedar, 1978).

Closely related to the issue of the development of lesbian-centered erotic imagery is that of woman-and-lesbian-centered models and norms of "good" sexual functioning. Tiefer (1979) has commented that for feminists studying women's sexual functioning, the Masters and Johnson model of sexual adequacy fails to desribe completely and speak to the experiences of many women. Tiefer specifically refers to the woman who by self-report is occasionally or never orgasmic, satisfied with her sexual functioning and is now under pressure, either from her partner or in response to her own doubts, to conform to the newest model of female sexual functioning put forth by the "experts." One must keep in mind that the concept of good female sexual functioning is a social construct that has varied enormously in the last century, going from a model in which the orgasmic woman was deviant and to be treated with clitoridectomies, to the current version in which the multi-orgasmic woman responding to clitoral stimulation is exhibiting "correct" and "healthy" behavior (Ehrenreich & English, 1978). The woman who is happy with a low level of desire, orgasm, or both, is as likely to be lesbian as heterosexual. My experience has been that for many such clients, the important intervention has been giving the client permission to see "healthy" sexual functioning in terms of whatever level of activity and interest she finds personally satisfying. Further, my work with lesbian clients has led me to believe that a model of sexual functioning that requires both partners to be equally active and orgasmic is not one that reflects either the reality or the needs of all lesbians. It is valuable for clients to have a therapist who supports them in creating models and strategies of sexual functioning that reflect the client's and the client's partner's own unique needs and preferences. Such strategies may include: (1) having one partner hold the other while the latter masturbates; (2) developing a relationship in which one partner is always the lover and the other always the one made love to; and (3) redefining the term "lovemaking" so that it describes behaviors that include neither genital touching nor orgasm on the part of either one or both partners. In short, the therapist can assist the client in discovering that her sexual functioning need not be a response to cultural stereotypes.

If one principle could guide the sex therapist in working with lesbians, it would be that of the absolute importance of therapist awareness of the many manifestations of internalized homophobia. One major function of sex therapy is that of anxiety reduction; internalized homophobia can act as a particularly potent and pernicious source of anxiety. And another important function of sex therapy is that of educating clients about sexuality. Internalized homophobia has created a well of ignorance that serves as a genuine barrier to many lesbians striving to create a comfortable, joyful level of sexual functioning.

Adjunct to this awareness regarding internalized oppression in clients is the need for heightened awareness on the part of the therapist regarding her or his own internalized homophobia. This self-inspection is particularly important for lesbian therapists. In order to provide clients with the best quality sex therapy possible, therapists must be certain within themselves that lesbian sexuality and lesbian relationships can be meaningful, joyful, and as imperfect in their own way as the best of those in the heterosexual realm. The lesbian therapist who is comfortable with her sexuality provides an important role model for the lesbian client struggling to claim her sexual self. Therapists must thus exercise caution in not projecting onto their clients their own personal fears and frustrations regarding sexuality. Therapists must also refrain from making their clients the proving ground in which heterosexual society is shown, for the therapists' benefit, that lesbianism is "better than" heterosexuality. In short, therapists must be aware that they, too have their own share of internalized homophobia, and must monitor it more carefully lest it be ignored when it conflicts with the therapists' external pronouncements and politics. Such a caveat would be unnecessary were it not for the many clients who have shared with me that they had encountered these dynamics in therapy with lesbian therapists.

Sex therapy with lesbian clients can be a positive and growth-producing experience for all involved. Both therapist and client have, in the context of sex therapy, an opportunity to examine, confront, and treat the effects of the most subtle and ingrained aspects of homophobia. This opportunity can best be realized when the effects of internalized oppression are identified and analyzed from the start of treatment.

REFERENCES

Barbach, L. (1976). *For yourself: The fulfillment of female sexuality.* New York: Anchor Books.
Califia, P. (1980). *Sapphistry: The book of lesbian sexuality.* Tallahassee, FL: Naiad Press.
Corinne, T. (1982). *Yantras of womanlove.* Tallahassee, FL: Naiad Press.
Ehrenreich, B., & English, D. (1978). *For her own good: 150 years of the experts' advice to women.* New York: Simon & Schuster.
Kaplan, H. S. (1979). *Disorders of sexual desire.* New York: Simon & Schuster.
Masters, W. H., & Johnson, V. E. (1978). *Homosexuality in perspective.* Boston: Little, Brown..
Memmi, A. (1965). *The colonizer and the colonized.* Boston: Beacon Press.
Nelly, & Cedar (1978). *A woman's touch: An anthology of lesbian erotica and sensuality.* Eugene, OR: Amazon Reality Collection.
Nomadic Sisters (1976). *Loving women.* Nomadic Sisters Publishing.
Sisley, E., & Harris, B. (1977). *The joy of lesbian sex.* New York: Simon & Schuster.
Tiefer, L. (1979, March). *A feminist perspective on women's sexuality.* Paper presented at the conference of the Association for Women in Psychology, Dallas.

Sexual Fulfillment
of Heterosexual, Bisexual,
and Homosexual Women

Lauren C. Bressler, MA
Abraham D. Lavender, PhD
Miami, Florida

ABSTRACT. Seventy females were interviewed in depth regarding their sexual responses and sexual fulfillment. They were categorized as heterosexual, bisexual, or homosexual according to self-definition. The quantity and quality of female sexual response, the source of the response, and the interactional patterns of sexuality were analyzed, and shown to differ, for different sexual orientations. The fallacy of emphasizing heterosexuality, and the fallacy of utilizing a heterosexual-homosexual dichotomy, in studies of female sexuality are indicated. It is suggested that knowledge about all sexual orientations can lead to more fulfilling sexuality in general, regardless of the individual's particular orientation.

Much of sexuality research assumes that there are only two sexual orientations; heterosexuality and homosexuality, and that only heterosexuality is important except when discussing deviant or alternative lifestyles. There is little research on bisexuality. Indeed, paraphrasing MacDonald (1981), to say there is a paucity of research on bisexuality is a gross understatement. Even when bisexuality has been recognized as reality, the tendency often has been to com-

Ms. Bressler completed her master's thesis in human sexuality, with a special interest in comparing the sexuality of heterosexuals, homosexuals, and bisexuals. She is active in public relations and consciousness raising groups regarding female sexuality.

Dr. Lavender is a clinical sociologist with a special interest in human sexuality. He has taught university courses in human sexuality for 10 years and has a special interest in societal factors that affect sexual functioning and dysfunctioning.

Research for this article was partially funded by the National Institute of Health, with sponsorship of the University of Miami. The authors wish to express special appreciation to Dr. Alvin W. Rose for his assistance in funding. Correspondence should be addressed to Dr. Lavender, 3066 Shipping Avenue, Miami, FL 33133.

bine bisexuality and homosexuality for research purposes. As De Cecco (1981) and MacDonald (1981) note, researchers, including Saghir and Robbins, Weinberg and Williams, Bell, and Masters and Johnson, analyze sexual orientation as dichotomized even when they have data indicating otherwise. In the words of LaTorre and Wendenburg (1983), bisexuals have "all too often, contaminated homosexual samples." Gonsiorek (1981) notes that 83% of Masters and Johnson's "homosexual" sample were actually bisexuals (Kinsey 2–4). Gonsiorek claims, as do these authors, that this causes serious problems with Masters and Johnson's conclusions.[1]

Even the research which recognizes distinctions among heterosexuality, bisexuality, and homosexuality often treats these categories as permanent, disparate, and value-laden. Little research treats the categories as potentially changing, possibly overlapping, and neutral.[2] Fewer researchers have conceptualized sexual orientation in such a manner as to ask: (a) the same individual about *both* same-gender and opposite-gender sexual experience; (b) allow the individual a self-definition of sexual orientation; (c) utilize at least a three-dimension categorization for data collection; and then (4) utilize this three-fold, nondisparate, self-defined categorization for analysis.

The works of Lavender and Bressler (1981) and LaTorre and Wendenberg (1983) are two exceptions to this latter point. Lavender and Bressler utilized a self-definition approach and compared the "philosophical perspectives" of heterosexual, bisexual, and homosexual women. The bisexuals and homosexuals had experiences with both same-gender and opposite-gender partners. They found that one's self-defined orientation is related to one's philosophy of life—that both heterosexuals and homosexuals tend to accept a dualistic or dichotomous perspective while bisexuals tend to accept a nondualistic perspective. LaTorre and Wendenburg utilized a self-definition and erotic preference approach and compared the psychological characteristics of bisexual, heterosexual, and homosexual women. All three groups in their study had both same-gender and opposite-gender experiences. They found that while 90.2% of the heterosexuals preferred sex with a man and 94.4% of the homosexuals preferred sex with a woman, 81.8% of the bisexuals had no preference.

The works of Lavender and Bressler and LaTorre and Wendenburg indicate strongly the fallacy of a heterosexual-homosexual dichotomy. The works of other researchers on individuals with specific orientations, e.g., Blumstein and Schwartz (1977), Fast and Wells (1975), Klein (1978), and Wolff (1971) on bisexuality, have helped in understanding sociological and psychological characteristics of individuals following specific sexual orientations.

While it is important to understand the sociological and psychological characteristics of individuals with different sexual orientations, there is increasing societal concern with sexual response and sexual fulfillment (Lavender, 1985). Studies of sexual response and sexual fulfillment, however, have suffered from the same limitations discussed earlier. While Masters and Johnson's (1979) research on homosexuality is the best known example of methodological and theoretical limitations, it is not an unusual example. And yet, the need for unbiased information specifically about sexual response is strong and applies not only to individuals in their personal lives, but also to education, counseling, and therapy.[3]

The concerns expressed above are even more relevant to females than to males, partly because of the limitations discussed above and partly because of a lack of sufficient research on female sexuality. Specific concern with female sexual response, and broader concern with female sexual fulfillment, is fairly recent, a result of changes in sexual values and increases in female consciousness. As a result, major biases remain in the study of female sexual response and fulfillment: (1) an emphasis on measuring quantity of orgasm, to the neglect of quality; (2) an emphasis on intercourse as the source of orgasm, to the neglect of other sources; and, (3) an emphasis on physical measures of orgasm, to the neglect of interactional (emotional and so on) aspects of sexuality.

The recent laboratory research on different types of orgasm has helped correct the first bias, but most of the field research continues to utilize quantity alone as a measure of sexual activity or fulfillment. Jayne (1981, p. 22) notes that with the exception of Fisher (1973), "all male researchers have approached female response quantitatively, not qualitatively." Related to this is the tendency to treat female orgasms in an all-or-none fashion, with women who consistently have orgasms being compared to those who don't have orgasms. As Jayne notes, "This either/or approach may have been fostered by the conceptualization of orgasm as an either/or phenomenon: either orgasm occurs or it does not" (p. 13). This all-or-none quantitative approach is not appropriate for female orgasms. Regarding the second bias, Masters and Johnson's laboratory research is a major exception to the intercourse emphasis, and the still-controversial work on the G-Spot has added a new dimension (Ladas, Whipple, & Perry, 1982). Comfort (1972) has suggested different techniques for heterosexuality, and Silverstein and White (1977) have done the same for homosexuality. Despite their popularity, however, these latter works have done little to change the research emphasis. In general, sexuality research has emphasized only masturbation as an alternative to intercourse (deBruijn, 1982). Despite the suggestions of some researchers that "technique does make a relatively important contribution" to female orgasm (deBruijn), the second bias generally remains in sexuality research. Even when researchers are concerned with quality as well as with quantity, and with different techniques, the third bias often remains. Emphasis is put on physiological measures of quantity or quality. And yet, "Women's reports of their subjective experiences with orgasm support the idea that orgasmic experience is a complex process having emotional and mental, as well as physical, components" (Bentler & Peeler, 1979, p. 419). The relationship between sexual and nonsexual behavior has generally not been dealt with systematically (Delehanty, 1982). The context in which the sexuality takes place and the mutuality of the interaction are also important.

While some researchers have commented on and attempted to correct these three biases, the almost exclusive reliance on heterosexuality for studies of female orgasm, and the dichotomizing of sexuality into heterosexuality and homosexuality, has encouraged the perpetuation of these biases. The purpose of this paper is to help correct these three biases by studying heterosexual, bisexual, and homosexual females, and to focus on sexual response and sexual fulfillment.

METHOD

This study is methodologically different from previous studies in that it combines all five of the following characteristics: it utilizes a self-labeling rather than a researcher's categorization of sexual orientation, presents comparative data rather than presenting data on only one orientation, compares three orientations rather than utilizing a hetero-sexual-homosexual dichotomy, provides in-depth data on women, and focuses on sexual response and sexual fulfillment rather than on sociological or psychological characteristics of individuals, or both.

The findings reported in this article are based on in-depth interviews with 23 women who labeled themselves as heterosexual, 22 women who labeled themselves as bisexual, and 25 women who labeled themselves as homosexual.[4] Respondents were obtained in a large southeastern metropolitan community through women's groups, colleges, personal contacts of the female author, referrals, and participation of the female author in a gay/straight consciousness raising group. The average respondent was 30 years of age, unmarried, had about 15 years of formal education, was in the middle-income range, and held moderate-to-liberal beliefs on political and social issues. The three groups did not differ significantly on important background variables.

The female author interviewed all the subjects, utilizing open-ended and semi-structured questions. Questions covered information on such areas as childhood development, sexual histories with males and females, negative sexual experiences, sexual techniques, and the relationship between emotional and physical aspects of sexuality and lovemaking. The average length of an interview was approximately 3 1/2 hours. The subjects' willingness to talk about sexuality, the amount of time required to conduct the interviews, and the use of women's groups and con-

sciousness raising groups affect the representative nature
of the sample. However, these factors lead to subjects
who may have given a great deal of thought to their sexuality and may therefore be more likely to be knowledgeable and incisive about their sexuality. Generalization
is limited because of the sample, but comparisons are possible within these groups, and findings are suggestive of
differences between heterosexuality, bisexuality, and homosexuality. This study had the advantages of in-depth
interviews and of basically equal sample sizes for the
three groups.

A maximum of four long-term relationships were analyzed for each subject. Long-term relationships were defined as those which lasted a minimum of 6 months with
sexual interaction. Two (8.7%) heterosexuals had experienced sexual interaction with females, but neither had had
a long-term relationship. Hence, all heterosexuals discussed up to four long-term relationships with men. When
applicable, bisexuals and homosexuals discussed two long-
term relationships with men and two long-term relationships with women. If a bisexual or homosexual had had
only one long-term relationship with one gender and three
or more long-term relationships with the other gender,
then that respondent discussed the one relationship with
one gender and three relationships with the other gender.
If a respondent had had less than four long-term relationships, then she discussed as many as she had experienced.
If a respondent had had more than four long-term relationships, then the four longest relationships were discussed.
The average number of long-term relationships per subject
was 2.60 for heterosexuals, 3.22 for bisexuals, and 2.96 for
homosexuals. One-way-analysis of variance and difference-
of-means tests were utilized to analyze the data.

FINDINGS

Quantity and Quality of Female Responses. As shown in
Table 1, heterosexual respondents averaged 4.7 orgasms per
week, bisexual respondents averaged 8.8, and homosexual
respondents averaged 6.2. The bisexual-heterosexual differ-

Table 1

Orgasms Averaged Per Week, And Descriptions of Orgasms, For Heterosexuals, Bisexuals, and Homosexuals

Sexual Orientation	Orgasms Per Week	Percent Describing Orgasms as "Strong"
Heterosexuals (n=23)	4.7*	48%**
Bisexuals (n=22)	8.8	86%
Homosexuals (n=25)	6.2	80%

*Heterosexual:Bisexual, t=2.27, < .05 **Heterosexual:Bisexual, t=3.44,< .01
 Heterosexual:Homosexual, t=.95, N.S.   Heterosexual:Homosexual, t=3.21,< .01
 Bisexual:Homosexual, t=1.41, < .20   Bisexual:Homosexual, t=.39, N.S.

ence was significant at the .05 level; the bisexual-homosexual difference was significant at only the .20 level. Heterosexuals and homosexuals did not differ from each other.[5] From Table 1, it is seen that qualitative differences also exist according to one's orientation. Bisexuals (86%) and homosexuals (80%) were significantly more likely than heterosexuals (48%) to use the word "strong" to describe their orgasms: "Mostly long and strong. They are very strong. Multiple orgasms are not as strong, just strung out. Tension is building and then it is released. They are mostly deep and long." Another marked difference according to sexual orientation occurs in the general process of building up to an orgasm: "It builds up and then there is an edge, and having an orgasm is going over that edge. Almost an explosion. Then it mellows out. Strong—satisfying." Only 3 heterosexuals (13%), compared to 9 bisexuals (40%) and 10 homosexuals (40%) referred to this building up process. Again, as with strength of orgasmic responses, few heterosexuals had such responses, while bisexuals and homosexuals had similarly high responses.

These findings must be interpreted with caution, for neither frequency nor strength—when compared to expectations, nonsexual interactions, and so forth—may be the important factor in sexual satisfaction. Additionally, even if one accepts the isolated importance of frequency and strength of orgasms, the fact that homosexuals reported fewer orgasms than bisexuals, but a similar quality of orgasms, could be interpreted two ways. Regarding homosexuals, it could be that it is "quality, not quantity, that counts." Or, regarding bisexuals, it could be said that "more is better." These findings, and differing possible interpretations, do indicate the need for more attention to be given to quality as well as quantity, and to the part that sexual orientation plays in both. Subsequent analyses, controlling for partner gender, resulted in patterns similar to the total sample for both frequency and strength.

Source of Female Response. As Table 2 shows, women of different sexual orientations do differ in relative importance of different techniques, but the overall differences are not significant. Bisexuals and homosexuals are similar in putting most emphasis on oral sexuality, followed by manual sexuality, whereas heterosexuals put primary emphasis on intercourse. With this major expected exception, however, heterosexuals then follow a pattern similar to that of bisexuals and homosexuals in putting emphasis on oral sexuality and manual sexuality. The other major exception to the overall pattern is the emphasis put on rubbing by homosexuals. But these findings do indicate that the heavy emphasis put on intercourse by researchers is incorrect for all orientations, and particularly for generalizing to bisexuality and homosexuality. The overall findings regarding the sexual fulfillment of bisexuals and homosexuals, as compared with that of heterosexuals, suggest that more research attention to bisexual and homosexual interactions would support a change of focus from intercourse to more varied techniques for sexual fulfillment. Controlling for partner gender, subsequent analyses resulted in patterns similar to the total sample.

Interaction With Partners. As shown in Table 3, a high percentage of respondents of all three orientations had experienced undesired behavior from their partners, behavior which emphasized the partner's physical (or personal) satisfaction rather than the mutual interaction of the two partners. Unlike the other two areas discussed, however, with this topic it is necessary to look at results separately for male and female partners. It is obvious that differences in interactional behavior do not depend primarily on sexual orientation, but rather on the gender of the partner. Male partners exhibit more undesired domineering behavior

Table 2

Sexual Techniques Utilized by Heterosexuals, Bisexuals, and Homosexuals

| Sexual Orientation | Number of Minutes and Percent of Total Time Utilized for Each Technique in Average Sexual Interaction | | | | |
	Oral	Manual	Intercourse	Vibrators	Rubbing
Heterosexuals (n=23)	9 (24.6%)	8 (21.9%)	19 (52.1%)	1/2 (1.4%)	0 (0.0%)
Bisexuals (n=22)	28 (40.0%)	21 (30.0%)	14 (20.0%)	3 (4.3%)	4 (5.7%)
Homosexuals (n=25)	15 (35.7%)	12 (28.6%)	5 (11.9%)	2 (4.8%)	8 (19.0%)

F=.86, N.S.

Table 3

Undesired Domineering Behavior Experienced by Heterosexuals,
Bisexuals, and Homosexuals

Sexual Orientation	# Experiencing Behavior			Percent of Respondents Experiencing Behavior
	Male Partners	Female Partners	Total	
Heterosexuals (n=23)	20	na	20	87%
Bisexuals (n=22)	16	1	17	77%
Homosexuals (n=25)	14	2	16	65%

Heterosexual:Bisexual, t=.71, N.S.
Heterosexual:Homosexual, t=1.94, < .10
Bisexual:Homosexual, t=1.14, N.S.

than do female partners. Not only did a high percentage of heterosexuals, who had long term relations only with males, experience such behavior, but nearly all of such behavior experienced by bisexuals and by homosexuals was experienced with male partners. There were 17 reportings of undesired behavior by bisexual females; 16 with male partners and 1 with a female partner. There were 16 reportings of such behavior by homosexuals; 14 with male partners and 2 with female partners. Statistically, 39% of the relationships with a male involved at least 1 incident of such behavior, while only 3% of the relationships with a female involved such behavior. These findings suggest that it is this area, nonsexual interaction, that may require even more research in the future. These findings, combined with Saliba's (1980) findings that bisexuals and homosexuals put more relative emphasis on affection than do heterosexuals, suggest that the interaction between sexual orientation, gender of partner, and sexual fulfillment is more complex in this area than in other areas.

DISCUSSION

The quantity and quality of female sexual response, the source of response, and the interactional patterns of sexuality differ depending on sexual orientation. With interactional patterns, the compounding factor of partner gender is also shown. The differences between heterosexuals, bisexuals, and homosexuals clearly indicate the fallacy of utilizing only heterosexuals in female sexuality studies. Furthermore, while there are similarities between homosexuals and bisexuals in this study which set them apart from heterosexuals, there are also sufficient differences to justify, even from a purely pragmatic perspective, separate attention to all three categories. The tendency to omit bisexuality as a category from sexuality studies is particularly unfortunate in view of the level of sexual fulfillment of bisexuals indicated in this study.

The analysis for this paper has been based on empirical findings, but attention to qualitative parts of the study point out even more the need for further research comparing sexual orientation utilizing the methodological approaches of this study. As indicated by certain quotations, it is possible that some women are more attuned to women's bodies, and that it is difficult for some men to learn what some women might already know: "I prefer women. Women are more attuned to my bodily reactions. It is something that is learned for a man. If he doesn't know, it is hard to teach. Women know each other's bodies better, and it feels natural and comfortable to be with a woman." Men and women have different sexual anatomies, different acculturations, and often different expectations. As Peplau (1981) states, "The character of a particular relationship may depend less on whether the partners are homosexual or heterosexual than on whether they are men or women" (p. 29). The works by Symons (1979) and by Paul and Weinrich (1982) indicate the theoretical and methodological questions still unanswered in this area. Depending on the emotional and physical preferences of the people involved, sexuality between partners of the opposite gender might require a compromise that sexuality between partners of the same gender does not require. Indeed, there may be physical preferences that can be fulfilled only, or at least more pleasurably, through a partner of one gender or the other. Ladas, Whipple, and Perry (1982) have come close to suggesting this in discussing anal sexuality in male-male relationships.

On the other hand, there has been little effort thus far on the part of either females or males to learn what most satisfies one's partner, regardless of the orientation or gender of the partner. It is possible, as indicated by other quotations in this study, that gender-stereotyped behavior has an important effect on sexual orientation, and that less gender-sterotyped behavior could have a different effect: "I don't like to have intercourse with men. With women it is more sensual. They are more into getting off on you. Not just their orgasm. They relate on a more intimate and tender level. Also, they are not so genitally oriented." Peplau (1981), for example, states that one of the major advantages mentioned by those who participate in same-gender sexuality is that they are freed from the traditional male-female role restrictions and allowed to interact simply as two people. It is possible that less gender-stereotyped sexuality might remove some of the communication problems between women and men and lead to more fulfilling heterosexuality. On the other hand, as people relate to each other as people without rigid gender role-playing, the result might be more flexibility and more fulfilling sexuality in general without regard to the orientation or gender of one's partner. We can only speculate at this point on these different possible outcomes; the need for more research is obvious.

Research has shown (LaTorre & Wendenburg, 1983), however, that women of all orientations are similar to each other in psychological characteristics, and that in many cases heterosexuals and homosexuals have the same values and experiences regarding sexuality and love (Peplau, 1981). This paper attempts to show how sexual interaction, including both emotional and physical dimensions, differs for women of different orientations. More knowledge about all orientations can help lead to more fulfilling sexuality in general, regardless of orientation, and in turn, sexuality in general can benefit from knowledge about what leads to sexual fulfillment. More knowledge needs to be obtained from studies of homosexuality, bisexuality, and female sexuality to complement knowledge gained from studies of heterosexuality and male sexuality.

NOTES

1. As a sex educator/clinician specializing in sexual dysfunctions, the senior author of this paper gives much (but not total) credence to the pioneering research of Masters and Johnson. He believes, however, that their conclusions about homosexuality are unreliable because of their dichotomy.

2. This state of affairs is particularly unfortunate because most sex researchers are presumably familiar with Kinsey, Pomeroy, and Martin's (1948) and Kinsey, Pomeroy, Martin, and Gebhard's (1953) multiple ratings and with their conclusions that sexual orientation can vary over a lifetime, and sometimes in a short period of time.

3. Most college textbooks continue to organize their presentation of topics in such a manner that the unsophisticated reader can infer that bisexuality and homosexuality belong together. This is sometimes based on acceptance of a dichotomous heterosexual-homosexual approach, with anyone having same-gender experiences (bisexuals) being classified as homosexual. Sometimes it is based on the belief that bisexuality and homosexuality are both alternative lifestyles. Regardless of the reason, the idea of heterosexuality versus bisexuality/homosexuality is reinforced. From a counseling or therapeutic perspective, it is important that counselors and therapists understand different types of sexuality, even if one does not agree that the therapist should necessarily have the same orientation as the client (Rochlin, 1981/82). This understanding is often lacking.

4. The data in this article represent a small part of the total data from the in-depth interviews. See Lavender and Bressler (1981) for other data. Analysis of the data is continuing.

5. A particularly interesting finding is that bisexuals report their average sexual interaction to last 70 minutes, while heterosexuals report an average of 36.5 minutes and homosexuals report an average of 42 minutes. While length of total interaction is not an emphasis of this article, these figures suggest the need for more attention to this topic.

REFERENCES

Bentler, P. M., & Peeler, W. H. (1979). Models of female orgasm. *Archives of Sexual Behavior*, 8, 405–423.

Blumstein, P. W., & Schwartz, P. (1977). Bisexuality: Some social psychological issues. *Journal of Social Issues, 33*, 30–45.

Comfort, A. (1972). *The joy of sex*. New York: Simon & Schuster.

deBruijn, G. (1982). From masturbation to orgasm with a partner: How some women bridge the gap—and why others don't. *Journal of Sex and Marital Therapy, 8*, 151–167.

De Cecco, J. P. (1981). Definition and meaning of sexual orientation. *Journal of Homosexuality, 6(4)*, 51–67.

Delahanty, R. (1982). Changes in assertiveness and changes in orgasmic response occurring with sexual therapy for preorgasmic women. *Journal of Sex and Marital Therapy, 8*, 198–208.

Fast, J., & Wells, H. (1975). *Bisexual living*. New York: Basic Books.

Fisher, S. (1973). *The female orgasm*. New York: Basic Books.

Gonsiorek, J. C. (1981). Review of *Homosexuality in Perspective* by W. H. Masters and V. E. Johnson. *Journal of Homosexuality, 6(3)*, 81–88.

Jayne, C. (1981). A two-dimensional model of female sexual response. *Journal of Sex and Marital Therapy, 7*, 3–30.

Kinsey, A. C., Pomeroy, W. B., Martin, C. E., & Gebhard, P. E. (1953). Sexual behavior in the human female. Philadelphia: W. B. Saunders.

Kinsey, A. C., Pomeroy, W. B., & Martin, C. E. (1948). *Sexual behavior in the human male*. Philadelphia: W. B. Saunders.

Klein, F. (1978). *The bisexual option*. New York: Arbor House.

Ladas, A. K., Whipple, B., & Perry, J. D. (1982). *The G-spot and other recent discoveries about human sexuality*. New York: Holt, Rinehart, & Winston.

LaTorre, P. A., & Wendenburg, K. (1983). Psychological characteristics of bisexual, heterosexual, and homosexual women. *Journal of Homosexuality, 9(1)*, 87–97.

Lavender, A. D. (1985). Societal influences on sexual dysfunctions: The clinical sociologist as sex educator. *Clinical Sociology Review, 3*, 129–142.

Lavender, A. D., & Bressler, L. (1981). Nondualists as deviants: Female bisexuals compared to female heterosexuals-homosexuals. *Deviant Behavior, 2*, 155–165.

MacDonald, A. P., Jr. (1981). Bisexuality: Some comments on research and theory. *Journal of Homosexuality, 6(3)*, 21–35.

Masters, W. H., & Johnson, V. E. (1979). *Homosexuality in Perspective*. Boston: Little, Brown.

Paul, W., & Weinrich, J. D. (1982). *Homosexuality: Social, psychological, and biological issues*. Beverly Hills: Sage Publications.

Peplau, W. A. (1981, March). What homosexuals want in a relationship. *Psychology Today*, pp. 28–38.

Rochlin, M. (1981/82). Sexual orientation of the therapist and therapeutic effectiveness with gay clients. *Journal of Homosexuality, 7(2/3)*, 21–29.

Saliba, P. (1980). *Variability in sexual orientation*. Unpublished master's thesis, San Francisco State University.

Silverstein, C., & White, E. (1977). *The Joy of gay sex*. New York: Crown.

Symons, D. (1979). *The evolution of human sexuality*. New York: Oxford University Press.

Wolff, C. (1971). *Love between women*. New York: St. Martins's Press.

Lesbian History:
A History of Change and Disparity

Myriam Everard
Leiden, The Netherlands

In the debate on the conceptualization of lesbianism, the central assumption is that homosexuality, male and female, is a historical category. That is to say, confining myself to the lesbian, the lesbian as we know her today characterized by her exclusive sexual preference for women, her own personal history, appearance, and psychological make-up—in short, her own identity—is a relatively recent historical figure, dating from the end of the 19th century.

At present this debate shows a growing consensus as to the historical relevance of two issues: first, the medical science of the second half of the 19th century which in the nosological fervor of the time defined "homosexuality" as one of the sexual perversions, and second, the romantic friendship. This romantic friendship, hitherto mainly described in Anglo Saxon countries, is described as the passionate and sensual, but non-sexual, love relationship between two women. This friendship between kindred spirits flourished in the sex-segregated, homosocial society of the 19th century, in which women were economically but not necessarily emotionally dependent upon men. This romantic friendship was seen as ennobling and worthwhile, and was socially fully acceptable.

Such friendship poses the question of the relation be-

Myriam Everard is a clinical psychologist who has published several articles on the Dutch history of lesbianism, and lectured on this same subject both in The Netherlands and Germany. She was the co-organizer of in the international conference "Among Men, Among Women" which was held at the University of Amsterdam in June 1983.

This article was originally presented at the conference "Among Men, Among Women." Thanks go to Sarah van Walsum for the present translation. Reprint requests may be sent to the author at Plantage 6, 2311 JC Leiden, The Netherlands.

tween the homosocial and homosexual, or between the "female world of love and ritual" (Carroll Smith Rosenberg) and the female homosexual's world of lust and male attire. In the work of Lillian Faderman this relation has already been defined as a chronological one: the homosocial antedates the homosexual, or more specifically, at the turn of the century romantic friendship was transmuted into female homosexuality by the machination of medical science.

Researching the history of the constitution of female homosexuality in the Netherlands, I will examine whether similar direct links are traceable in Dutch history. The first question to be answered is: Do the 19th century Netherlands reveal anything resembling this romantic friendship, or did other ways of relating exist among women? This leads to the second question: What is the relation between medical science and these ways of relating among women, or more specifically, is the homosexual woman of the 20th century the medical transformation of the 19th century romantic friend?

That a Dutch equivalent to the romantic friendship existed at the end of the 18th century in the *zielsvriendschap* or *hartsvriendschap*[1] can be gathered out of the work and life of Aagje Deken, who lived from 1741 till 1804. She is well known in Dutch literary history through her relationship with Betje Wolff, who lived from 1738 to 1804, with whom she wrote several books and shared a good deal of her life. Deken was the daughter of well-to-do parents, who both died when Aagje was 4 years old. She was then placed in the orphanage of the Collegianten in Amsterdam. These Collegianten formed an intellectual elite among the various Protestant sects. They stressed the personal experience of faith, freedom of speech, a mutual tolerance bridging the various religious convictions of the day, and the practice of virtue.

In 1775, Deken published *Stichtelijke Gedichten*[2] (Edifying Verse), a volume of poems compiled by Aagje from her and Maria Bosch's works after Bosch's death. A great number of poems concern the zielsvriendschap between Aagje Deken and Maria Bosch, a few concern two other zielsvriendschappen of hers: with Maria Bavink and with

Elisabeth Schreuders. Some fragments from a poem to Maria Bavink include:

> No David could woo his Jonathan more
> Than our hearts have wooed each other.
> How sweet 't would be, as true souls' friends
> To strive for the dearest blessing of all
> From God, the greatest of all Friends
> (. . .) May I live forever
> Next to her with whom my Heart's already joined.
> Then could we prove to all the world
> Despite those who dare scorn at Friendship
> That she still dwells amongst us here![3]

The friendship which Aagje extols in these verses is a true and lasting spiritual bond, a joining of two souls that together reach for the elevated and resist all worldly attachments. It is a love without passion, but not without fire, as Aagje puts it. Her ideal, a *zielsvriendin* with whom to share the rest of her life and eventually her grave, was not easily realized. Her first friend, Maria Bavink, left her in 1769 after 10 years of friendship in the orphanage, indeed under the pressure of economic necessity to enter into domestic service. Aagje lived together with her second friend, Maria Bosch, until the latter's death in 1773. Her third friend, Elisabeth Schreuders, she lost after 3 years to a man. Finally, she and Betje Wolff spent the last 27 years of both their lives together, earned their living together writing, and in the end were buried together.[4]

In short, the zielsvriendschap Aagje Deken strove for all her life has much in common with the "romantic friendship" described. A friendship, however, that bears a conspicuous religious element which is not, I believe, without significance. Clearly not in accordance with the self-evident and socially accepted character of a romantic friendship is the fact that Aagje, on more than one occasion, felt obliged to justify her friendship with Maria Bosch, first of all to God, but also to a world that thought such a love "insipid, mean and disgusting."

This zielsvriendschap cannot be attributed solely to a personal preference of Aagje's, but was common among women of her time and standing, as appears in the work of her contemporary, Elisabeth Maria Post.

Elisabeth Maria Post, born in 1775 into a family of notaries, died in 1812, and married at an advanced age to a minister, was the author of a number of books. One of these is *Het Land* (The Countryside) published in 1788,[5] an epistolary novel composed for a large part of the correspondence between two friends. They refer to themselves as *hartsvriendinnen*. Emilia lives alone in the country, Eufrosyne with her mother in the city. Both are about 25 years old. The exchange of letters begins at the start of their friendship and ends with Eufrosyne's premature death less than a year later. The growing friendship they feel for each other leads to numerous confessions and reflections in which the same themes that characterized the zielsvriendschap of Aagje Deken can be found: the spiritual bond, the united effort to surpass baser emotions, the longing to live together and to be united in death. During one of Eufrosyne's visits to the countryside they discuss the differences between friendship between women and love between men and women:

> Eufrosyne to Emilia:
>
> Oh! What a wonderful mixture of emotions transports me! I feel nature! I feel friendship! How strongly my entire soul rejoices in both! Truly Emilia, I believe friendship is stronger than love!
>
> Thereupon Emilia answers:
>
> What is love without friendship to steer it? An animal instinct, an unstable loose passion, as far removed from the pure delights of friendship as it is surpassed by its nobility. I shrink from the thought of a union based on such love, and not on the unison of two souls.[6]

This moral superiority of a lasting spiritual bond over transient bodily lust, coupled with a religiously inspired search for spiritual perfection, fit remarkably well into Victorian sexual ideology of the passionlessness of middle class women as analyzed by Nancy Cott.[7] Victorian Christian morality, which is traditionally regarded as hostile towards women and responsible for the asexuality of Victorian women, was apparently transformed by these women into a source of strength, independence, and mutual support.

While the well-to-do, educated women of the middle class were practicing to "quell the passions of the flesh" as Aagje Deken put it, different things were happening among women from another social category. Between 1792 and 1798 there were five court cases in Amsterdam in which a total of 12 women were charged for "foul sodomitical behavior."[8] Practically all of these women were from the lowest social strata—street vendors, prostitutes, women with no sure means of support. Most of them were sturdy drinkers and some would even saunter through the streets dressed as men. Economic necessity did not force these women apart; on the contrary, through economic necessity they were often obliged to share the same bed. These women apparently turned to each other rather than to men, not because they were repelled by male preoccupations with physical lust, but because they didn't need men to satisfy their own desires. Clearly, the concept zielsvriendschap does not include the irregular sexual relationships between these women. Before drawing any conclusions, however, we must continue into the 19th century to see if and how the zielsvriendschap continued to manifest itself.

Taking a large step, I arrive at Catharina Alberdingk Thijm.[9] Born in 1848 of a literary family, she managed for the better part of her life to earn her living with her writing. As was common among people of her standing, she attended boarding school abroad. The life of the marriageable daughter she was obliged to lead after completing her studies did not agree with her, and she decided to enter a convent. This convent closed after 8 years, and she stepped out of the order. She was then 29 years old. After having worked for a number of years as a governess, very unusual work in those times for a woman of her means, she became acquainted with Lady Louise Stratenus, with whom she would live and work for the next 14 years. This friendship ended when Catharina became engaged at the age of 46 for what turned out to be a short-lived betrothal. The next year Catharina, together with her friend at that time, Jacoba van Zoelen, established a house in Amsterdam for homeless women and children, which they had to close after 5 years due to lack of funds. She died a few years later in 1908.

Rather than going further into Alberdingk's life story and her friendships with women, I would like to direct my attention to her work, in particular to the journal she started in 1882 and whose contents, for a while, flowed entirely from her pen: *Lelie- en Rozenknoppen* (Lily- and Rosebuds), a weekly magazine for girls.[10]

Catharina was chief editior of *Lelie- en Rozenknoppen* for 5 years. This magazine was intended, as she herself put it, for young ladies "of better and wealthier standing." The educational character of the magazine is evident: the feature articles encouraged the readers to practice numerous virtues such as patience, endurance, and obedience, particularly toward their mothers. It was also very class-bound: Rules regarding etiquette, appearance, clothing, and so forth were regularly expounded on in such articles as "Our Teeth and Nails," "How Well-bred Young Ladies Eat and Drink," "Whispering and Listening," and so forth. Topics of a completely different kind were also dealt with, such as biographies of famous women artists like Sarah Bernhardt, already very "unedifying" for the male roles she played, and the French painter Rosa Bonheur, who dressed as a man, lived with a woman, and—not mentioned in the said biography—donated her autobiography to Hirschfeld for his collection of sexual variants. There was even a series of articles devoted to women who had served in the army while dressed as men.

What's more, through the years Catharina gave the impression of deliberately striving for a close bond of friendship between herself and her young readers. She addressed them very personally, especially in the more educational articles, and thus created a sphere of intimacy. This is particularly evidenced by the busy correspondence she carried on with her subscribers. She answered the letters not only through her column, but also in person, and regularly exchanged portraits. She also organized excursions to exhibitions and arranged private meetings. She even ran an office for this purpose. It isn't surprising then to see that every year she devoted a number of leading articles to the topic of friendship. This type of friendship closely resembled the zielsvriendschap as described by Aagje Deken and Elisabeth Post almost a century earlier.

True friendship was that close and lasting bond, based on love, trust, and respect, in which two women endure and correct each other's faults in order to help each other to become good and noble women. For this friendship, this "most precious thing in a woman's life," Catharina still used the name of zielsvriendschap.

In comparison, what is known of what took place on the other side of the social-economic dividing line? Here again we must rely upon indirect sources of information. Where earlier a courtroom provided the scenery, we are now faced with an insane asylum. But despite the change in setting, the play remains the same.

In 1882 an article appeared in the medical literature on so-called "insania moralis,"[11] containing a description of Magdalena van W. This was apparently a textbook case, since she also appeared in an article on moral insanity in 1891.[12] The doctors provided the following information concerning her background. Magdalena was born in 1863, one of a family of children of whom she was the only one to survive childhood. Her father was a bricklayer, her mother of illegitimate birth. Sent away from every school because of her unmanageable behavior, Magdalena led a life of vagrancy and street fighting. This brought her quickly into Talita Kumi, a children's home connected to an asylum for fallen women. No sooner was she released than she resumed her old life of roaming, brawling, thievery, and prostitution, which brought her into regular contact with police and corrective institutions.

In those days heavy debates were being carried on concerning the categorization of insanity. One of the categories which emerged out of these discussions was the so-called "insania moralis" or moral insanity. Insania moralis is described by the psychiatrist Van Deventer, the first to write about Magdalena, as a flaw in the moral sensibilities which need not be accompanied by any intellectual de-

fects. Characteristic for those who suffered insania moralis
were, as he declared:

> excesses in Venere and in Baccho, perverse tenden-
> cies, theft, dishonesty, perfidy, laziness, cruelty, va-
> grancy and a complete shamelessness . . . they spend
> much of their lives in corrective institutions, prisons,
> etc., usually without any effect.[13]

Magdalena displayed all of these symptoms. Her sexual
behavior also betrayed her ailment, as Van Deventer
demonstrated:

> [She] has the habit of holding her hands to her genitals
> at night, and even went so far as to invite her aunt,
> with whom she shared a bed . . . and even to try to
> force her to do it together as man and woman.[14]

The following statement may serve as an illustration of
the gap which separated Magdalena from her middle-class
contemporaries.

> As a housemaid she received notice because she
> shared her bed with a female friend; there were many
> complaints of her highly obscene language and man-
> ners . . . Several ladies were so upset by her behavior
> that medical assistance had to be called for.[15]

In short, just as the zielsvriendschap continued among the
well-to-do, so also the explicitly sexual relationships continued among lower-class women, as did the difference in
value attributed to both by society. This difference in
public appreciation, particularly among the medical profession, can also be illustrated by comparing the following
two incidents.

   In 1887, two women came to the Clinic for Psychotherapy in Amsterdam for treatment of nervous complaints.
This clinic, established by the psychiatrists Van Eeden and
Van Renterghem, offered hypnotic treatment of nervous
disorders to for the most part wealthy patients.

   Van Renterghem was able to relieve both women of

their complaints, without touching on their relationship, although he was clearly aware of its nature. In his words:

> Both ladies lived together, were "des inséparables," had renounced love, namely that for a man, gave each other the affection locked in their bosoms and lived contentedly.[16]

On the other side, in 1895 the city council of Amsterdam appointed a committee with instructions to investigate the nature and extent of prostitution in the city and to suggest public measures which could be taken. The report, brought out in 1897,[17] included two accounts written by two doctors who were members of the committee. For the present purposes, I shall limit myself to the account of Dr. Voûte, who reported on his investigations in the brothels among the prostitutes themselves.

Voûte presented 21 prostitutes, 6 madames and employers, and 1 mistress of a so-called plaçeur (a pander in prostitutes) with a questionnaire. This questionnaire consisted of 26 questions concerning their background, age, record, working conditions, and the age, status, and demands of their male customers, plus 7 questions concerning their own sexual habits, of which no less than 6 dealt with details of possible sexual relationships with other women. The answers of these questions are only briefly summarized in the account. Half of the prostitutes slept with another woman, and Voûte even learned that sometimes two of them performed together for money. Unfortunately, he wasn't sufficiently alert to ask about a possible female clientele. Who knows, but that perhaps the two divided worlds of zielsvriendschap and women's sex met in the brothel.

Returning to my first question, it is clear that in the Netherlands of the 19th century an equivalent to the romantic friend existed in the zielsvriendin. But it is equally obvious that this zielsvriendin could only be found in certain social strata, and that beyond those limits very different relations among women could exist. The question is: What is the connection between these different relationships and female homosexuality?, which in turn brings me to my second question: Did the manipulations of the medical profession transform the 19th century romantic friendship into 20th century female homosexuality?

The medical material currently at my disposal is by no means complete. I have up to now concentrated my research on the development of medical theory on female homosexuality in the Netherlands, as reflected in medical journals in the period between 1880 and 1940.[18] What follows now is therefore said with due caution.

In the Netherlands as in surrounding countries, various labels were applied for a number of years to same-sex love until "homosexuality" finally became the accepted term. The discussion started in 1883 with an article by Donkersloot on the "clinical-forensic interpretation of perverse sexual urge."[19] After this, the number of theoretical essays, case studies, confessions, book reviews, and debates on the subject increased steadily. It would take 45 years, however, before the first woman would come into the picture. She doesn't make her appearance until 1929, in the Dutch Journal for Medical Science, and we receive only a glimpse of her at that. In an account of a meeting of neurologists, a "discussion concerning homosexuality in a young girl" by the psychoanalyst Blok is reported. The account of this discussion is very brief.

> Speaker exhibits a young girl, aged fifteen years, whose behaviour and pursuits were exactly those of a boy. Her body is typically female. On the basis of the psycho-analytic literature he traces the mechanism that may have triggered these symptoms.[20]

In those days, the medical profession was, in the Netherlands as elsewhere, split into two camps on the issue of homosexuality, one side being those who regarded homosexuality as a largely psychological phenomenon with the implication that everyone could, under certain circumstances, develop into a homosexual, but that such a development could also be reversed. This interpretation leaned heavily on psychoanalysis. On the other side were those who saw homosexuality as a biological phenomenon, an inherent sexual variant which could be found among a small but fixed number of people and which no medic could alter. This interpretation was based largely on Hirschfeld's "Zwischenstufen" theory, which found many followers and supporters within Dutch homosexual emancipation circles.

It was this latter camp which in 1934 produced the second publication on homosexuality in which women also appeared: an article by Sanders, director of the department for medical-statistical research at the Dutch Institute for Research Into Human Heredity and Race Biology.[21] Sanders sought to prove that homosexuality was a genetically determined sexual variant, and resorted to the classical proof: the monozygotic twin. Of the eight twins he dealt with in this context (on whom he could lay hands, thanks to the collaboration of the Dutch Scientific Humanitarian Committee, the NWHK), one consisted of two sisters. They answered the classical description: always preferred boys' games to girlish amusements; never felt any sexual attraction to men, although they enjoyed their company; had deep manly voices, and preferred masculine occupations. They were evasive concerning their sexual relationships with women, but Sanders was informed that they associated with homosexual women and performed homosexual acts. All that was lacking was the "more or less fully developed beard" which, according to Sanders, characterized homosexual women.

Another article, from the psychoanalytical camp,[22] appeared in 1935, in which the psychoanalyst Westerman Holstijn described the close connection between paranoia and homosexuality, and illustrated this with a few case studies. One of these case studies concerned a woman, unmarried, born in 1893, from a modest background which she outgrew by gaining a number of professional promotions. She broke off an engagement at the age of 25 and shortly thereafter entered into an intimate friendship with a female colleague. The tokens of her friendship included passionate kisses and tender embraces, and her fondest wish was to spend the rest of her life with her beloved friend. This, however, was not to be: her friend got married. As a result, she fell into confusion, suffered hallucinations and delusions of being followed by men with dishonorable intentions, and was eventually confined to a mental asylum. The diagnosis was schizophrenia accompanied by paranoid delusions, with the added note that the patient displayed strong homosexual tendencies, of which she herself was not aware and which she unconsciously tried to cover with heterosexually colored anxieties.

Sixty years of Dutch medical probing into homosexuality yield a meager harvest. I realize it is difficult to draw any conclusions from only three medical descriptions of female homosexuality, except that for the present there can hardly be spoken of any direct medical offensive against independent "romantic friends." Only in the last case is it at all possible to speak of a "romantic friend" being accused, as it were, of homosexual tendencies. Yet it wasn't the fact that she so fondly embraced her friend or that she wished to live with her that brought the medics into action, but instead her inability to cope with a broken heart, an affliction which surely had nothing to do with the gender of the lost lover. So for the present, the answer to my second question, whether the 20th century homosexual woman is a medical transformation of the 19th century romantic friend, must be negative.

At one time it did look as though independent women in the Netherlands would be subjected to medical suspicions regarding their sexuality, that time being the late 19th century when so-called women's studies (in those days studying by women) formed the subject of a broad-based discussion which also included the medical profession. A number of doctors raised their voices in protest against women's studies, arguing that the sexual lives of women would suffer from intellectual exertion. In other words, women's studies would produce barren, asexual women, sterile workbees in the literal sense of the word: educated women who would give birth later, less frequently, or even not at all. In the opinion of these doctors, the result would be the downfall of the species, considering all those morally insane who would continue, unabated, to proliferate.[23] In short, what might have developed into an argument against female friendship proved to be nothing more than the eugenetic fears of the middle class, which also played its role in the medics' preoccupation with "insania moralis."

SUMMARY

In the 19th century Netherlands, different relationships among women appear to have been possible, social class being the differentiating factor. The Dutch equivalent of the "romantic friendship" was the zielsvriendschap, that love-relation between women in which both strove for the higher, for that spiritual bond which they believed far superior to the relation between men and women based on temporary sexual lust. During the 19th century that zielsvriendschap appears to have continued untouched and unchanged among women of the educated, well-to-do classes. Outside these circles, notably in the lower classes, women appear to have had passionate relationships with each other very much based on that temporary sexual lust, relationships branded with different consecutive labels by different disciplines; *sodomy* in a theological-judicial, *insania moralis* in a medical-judicial, regime.

The role of the medical profession in the emergence of female homosexuality in the Netherlands is as yet not very clear, but it does not seem, however, to have aimed at any morbidification of the zielsvriendschap.

If we cannot speak of a direct relation between romantic friendship and female homosexuality, how then can this relation be conceptualized? The medical profession, producer of the category "homosexuality," is neither as monolithic nor as uniform as it appears. Certainly in its practice it is marked by differences, and here again class is the differentiating factor: Asylums recruit their patients from other segments of the population than do the consulting rooms of the private psychoanalytic practitioner.

The medical profession first displayed an interest in sexual variants in general and homosexuality, male homosexuality in particular, in the second half of the 19th century. This interest developed within the context of court-room medicine and criminal anthropology. In this field of middle-class corrective agencies and lower-class sexual morality, scientists like Hirschfield intervened. They were men, to be sure, but with a high personal stake in the issue, far removed from a zeal to incriminate romantic friends. They presented a new concept, homosexuality, in an attempt to decriminalize sexual relations among men and among women, and postulated that homosexuality should not be seen as a form of degeneracy or punishable perversity, but as a biological variety, a congenital disposition which manifests itself both physically and psychologically through sexual inversion. The inverted woman thus was seen as a female with male sex characteristics, which explained her sexual preference for women. In the heat of scientific and emancipatory enthusiasm, as many examples as possible were brought together to support this theory. Of course, the search was conducted where it was likely to produce results; that is, not among romantic friends but among women who maintained sexual relationships with other women.

A few decades later in another branch of medical science, psychoanalysis, this image of the homosexual woman was renewed and elaborated on. The homosexual and the heterosexual are now no longer distinct biological categories; all people are basically bisexual. Whether one grows up to become a homosexual or a heterosexual depends on one's personal psychosexual development. All that distinguishes a homosexual from a heterosexual woman is her sexual object choice. There is no parallel between physical and psychic hermaphroditism and sexual preference, in other words: Women no longer have to display any male sex characteristics to be homosexual.

Clearly, the romantic friend could easily fit into this approach, certainly when one considers the middle-class origin of most psychoanalytic patients. And this indeed appears to have been the case when one considers Freud's publication *Uber die Psychogenese eines Falles von weiblicher Homosexualität* (1920). In this "case of homosexuality in a woman," the characteristics of the typical romantic friendship are unmistakeable: the upper-class origin of the 18-year-old girl, the concomitant attitude towards sex as something unaesthetic, and the passionate attachment to a lady aged 28, with all the wooing and tokens of tenderness a romantic friendship allowed for.

So if one wants to write lesbian history to look for the appropriate ancestor of today's lesbian, it is not so much the 19th century middle-class romantic friend as it is her housemaid of so-said "highly obscene language and manners" that appears to be her historical predecessor.

NOTES

1. Literally respectively "soul's friendship" and "hearts' friendship."
2. Maria Bosch en Agatha Deken, *Stichtelyke gedichten* (Amsterdam: Yntema & Tieboel, 1775). For a more detailed discussion of the life of Agatha Deken and her zielsvriendschappen, see: Myriam Everard, "Tribade of zielsvriendin," *Groniek, 77* (1982), pp. 16–20.
3. Fragment of a poem by Aagje Deken addressed to Maria Bavink, *Stichtelyke gedichten*, p. 133.
4. Aagje Deken outlived Betje Wolf by only 12 days.
5. Elisabeth Maria Post, *Het land, in brieven* (Amsterdam: Allart, 1778).
6. *Het land*, pp. 146–147.
7. See Nancy Cott, "Passionlessness: An interpretation of victorian sexual ideology," *Signs, 4* (1978), pp. 219–236.
8. See Theo van der Meer, "Liefkozeryen en vuyligheden," *Groniek, 66* (1980), pp. 34–37.
9. For the biographical data I rely on Marieke Van Driel & Ludi Zoomer, *Catharina Alberdingk Thijm, leven en werk* (Amsterdam: Universiteit van Amsterdam—Instituut voor Neerlandistiek, 1980, unpublished paper.)
10. This was not the only girl's journal she would start. In 1887 followed *De Hollandsche Lelie* and in 1888 *La jeune fille*, brought out in Belgium and under the title *Journal des jeunes filles* in France as well.
11. J. van Deventer Szn., "Bijdrage tot de diagnostiek van insania moralis," *Nederlandsch Tijdschrift voor Geneeskunde*, 1882, pp. 693–706.
12. P. Kok Ankersmit & J. van Deventer Szn., "Een forensisch geval van zedelijke krankzinnigheid," *Psychiatrische Bladen, IX* (1891), pp. 90–114.
13. Van Deventer (1882), pp. 693–694
14. Van Deventer (1882), p. 703.
15. Kok Ankersmit & Van Deventer (1891), p. 100.
16. A. W. van Renterghem, *Autobiographie II* (Amsterdam, 1927), p. 39.
17. Rapport der commissie uit den Amsterdamschen gemeenteraad over de prostitutiekwestie, met bijgevoegda nota's van Dr. Blooder en Dr. Voûte dd. 20 Januari 1897, RA-Amsterdam, inv.nr. 5136.
18. Viz. *Nederlandsch Tijdschrift voor Geneeskunde* (Amsterdam: Van Rossen, 1880–1940), *Nederlandsch Tijdschrift voor Verloskunde en Gynaecologie* (Haarlem: Bohn, 1889–1940), *Psychiatrische (en Neurologische) Bladen* (Dordrecht: Van Elk/Amsterdam: Van Rossen, 1883–1940) , *Psychiatrische-Juridisch Gezelschap* (Amsterdam: Van Rossen, 1907–1940). (Author: Insert year, publisher).
19. N. B. Donkersloot, "Klinisch-forensische beteekenis der perverse geslachtsdrift," *Geneeskundige Courant, 37* (1883), no. 8–14.
20. A. M. Blok, "Bespreking van een geval van homosexualiteit bij een jong meisje," *Nederlandsch Tijdschrift voor Geneeskunde*, 1929 I, p. 1296.
21. J. Sanders. "Homosexueele tweelingen," *Nederlandsch Tijdschrift voor Geneeskunde*, 1934 III, pp. 3346–3352.
22. A. J. Westerman Holstijn, "Zur Psychoanalyse der Paranoiker," *Psychiatrische en Neurologische Bladen, 31* (1935), pp. 359–428.
23. A position maintained by a.o. the psychiatrist C. Winkler in "De vrouw en de studie te midden der vrouwenbeweging," Hector Treub & C. Winkler, *De vrouw en de studie* (Haarlem: Bohn, 1898), p. 31–64.

Lesbians Over 65:
A Triply Invisible Minority

Monika Kehoe, PhD
San Francisco State University

ABSTRACT. Questionnaire responses from 50 lesbians, 65 to 85 years of age, were used to describe their present status, their educational background, their economic and occupational condition, their personal and psycho/social concerns, as well as their perception of their own physical and mental health. The data suggests that the 65+ lesbian is a survivor, a balanced personality, coping with aging in a satisfactory manner.

INTRODUCTION

Invisible as a female, aging, and deviant, ignored by gerontologists,[1] feminists,[2] even sexologists dealing specifically with homosexuality,[3] lesbians over 65 have been an unknown, mysterious minority. They are a social embarrassment to the wider community and the presumption has been—if anyone thought about it at all—that lesbians, as well as gay men, are either "cured" when they reach seniority or die young from alcoholism, suicide, or social diseases.

Berger (1982)[4] points out in the introduction to his book, *Gay and Gray*, that "there are nearly a million homosexual men over the age of 65 in our country today." If so, we can estimate that lesbians in the same age group, being longer-lived as women, must number well over a million, "most of whom have remained hidden to an even greater extent," as Berger admits, than their male counterparts. This, he points out, "is reflected in the newly emerging literature on the older homosexual, which

---

Correspondence should be addressed to the author, 87 Banks Street, San Francisco, CA 94110.

139

focuses primarily on the male. The older women are simply less accessible to the probing eye or the researcher." He goes on to explain, rather ruefully, "We were unable to collect sufficient information on the older lesbian and therefore decided to limit *Gay and Gray* to males."

Even when the research is limited to aging and lesbianism, as in the case of two Master's theses, (1) Chris Almvig's "The Invisible Minority: Aging and Lesbianism," at the New School, in New York City, in which only 12 female subjects over 65 years of age were included in her sample; and (2) the 1979 study of "The Older Lesbian" by Mina K. Robinson at California State University, Dominguez Hills, in which seven 65+ women were involved, the old-old women are neglected. This is not intended as a criticism of the pioneer research done by these scholars, but only a testimonial to the difficulty of reaching deeply closeted lesbians in this advanced age group. Indeed, as a matter of common usage among lesbians, "older" has usually meant *over 40*, since few beyond that age socialize within the lesbian community. Besides the Almvig and Robinson works, there have been several even earlier research efforts dealing with aging gays *and* lesbians, such as the Minnegerode and Adelman investigation (1970) of 6 males and 5 females between the ages of 60 and 77.

The *Starr-Weiner Report on Sex and Sexuality in the Mature Years* (1981–1982)[5] is typical of the sexologists' treatment of lesbianism and the elderly. There are only two references to lesbianism listed in the index: one on page 172 describes it as the proclivity of a "small, adventurous minority" of their sample; and, the other on page 182, in which the authors admit, somewhat apologetically, that a few of their subjects "are able to consider, if not participate in, maverick alternatives such as lesbianism."

Earlier surveys of homosexuals sometimes included a few lesbians, but seldom any over 40. These subjects were often studied in clinical or institutional settings and thus represent only an aberrant segment of the population under scrutiny. Of course, during earlier times when homosexuality was considered pathological and thus generally medicalized, it would have been difficult to get volunteers for observation any other way.[6] The accumulation of 50 completed questionnaires from lesbians over 65 is, therefore, probably the most extensive survey made to date of this specific age group of homosexual women.[7]

Another singular feature of the research reported here is its nationwide scope. In the previous studies of "older" lesbians, the sample has been regional, limited to one area of the country or representing mainly the metropolitan centers on either coast. The current survey, on the other hand, includes respondents living in all regions of the continental United States.[8]

The purpose of the present study was to examine the lives of 50 lesbians over 65. It was intended to be descriptive of their status, their educational background, their economic and occupational condition, their personal and psycho-social concerns, and to explore their perception of their own physical and mental health. It was designed to investigate their attitudes toward relationships, their hopes for the future, their needs, and the problems they face.

The *limitations* of this inquiry were many and included the homogeneity of the sample, a trouble which has plagued the research on homosexuality to date. All respondents were white, middle-class, well-educated, self-identified volunteers. All were likewise U.S. citizens. Although they were not representative of the entire population under review, the information gathered about them extends the scope of investigation of more individuals in a wider range of settings.[9] There were also many important omissions in the questionnaire, such as no query on hearing loss or impairment, omissions not discovered until brought to attention by a respondent. In some parts, the instrument was inadequately designed to elicit the information desired. Interviews could have mitigated many of the defects of the questionnaire, but lack of funds made such personal contact impossible. Reliability was undoubtedly affected by some respondents' generationally typical resistance to probing of such intimate and personal matters. As a result, their responses may have been, on occasion, equivocal or unreported.

METHOD

The procedure for gathering data was by solicitation: announcements in lesbian/feminist periodicals and newsletters, posters sent to feminist bookstores and women's centers, letters to directors of University of Women's Studies programs, notices to special interest groups dealing with "older" lesbians and to gay caucuses of academic associations, and word-of-mouth contacts. The announcements thus circulated described the project and requested those eligible to write or call if they were willing to participate. The letters sent to universities and other organizations also indicated the nature of the project and asked that the information be disseminated as widely as possible, again with a request for those who were eligible to respond. A total of 78 questionnaires were distributed, only to those requesting copies. Out of this number 28 were not returned.

This publicity campaign brought a surprising number of replies from individuals, some of whom said they were in their early 60's, not yet 65, but would like to help anyway, while others sent along the address of a friend over 65 who had agreed to participate. This "snowball" method of recruiting respondents resulted in a sample, as indicated above, of only white, well-educated women of relatively high social/economic status. Born in 18 states and 3 foreign countries, they live now in 23 states and the District of Columbia.

The questionnaire was printed[10] on both sides of 6 pages of light-blue, legal-size sheets of paper. It was mailed in a legal-size envelope with a cover letter[11] and a self-addressed, stamped envelope for its return.[12] It contained 161 items divided into the following categories: Demographics, Education, Personal and Psycho/Social Concerns, Economic and Occupational Status, Physical and Mental Health. The last two questions, #160, "What are the most serious problems you face now?", and #161, "How could a special social organization for older lesbians help?", were intended to give the respondents an opportunity to explain their most urgent needs and suggest solutions to their most pressing problems.

HIGHLIGHTS OF RESULTS

The respondents ranged in age from 65 to 85 years. Half, or 25, had at some time in their lives been in conventional male/female marriages ranging from 3 weeks to 44 years, but none was in such a union at the time of reporting; 21 never married, and 25 reported themselves as "unattached." The majority had no gay relatives that they knew of; 3 had gay daughters, 1 a gay son, and 6 had gay brothers. The majority had no children; 1 had 31 grandchildren.

Table I

Age Distribution of Respondents

Age	F
5–69	28
70–74	15
75–80	5
80–84	0
85–90	1
Unreported	1

In terms of education, 35 were college graduates and 25 had advanced degrees. All the "never married" were among those with advanced degrees. Under the heading of Personal and Psycho/Social Concerns, the majority reported a good self-image and felt positive about being identified as a lesbian. Sex was considered an integral part of a lesbian relationship by 33 of the respondents. The total sample included 7 bisexuals. Half met the first woman they were emotionally involved with in an educational setting, nearly three-fourths recognizing their lesbianism in their teens. At the time of reporting, the majority considered themselves not closeted, but indicated they did not belong to any lesbian social or professional groups. Contrary to expectations, there were few who admitted to being, or ever having been, "jocks." Most had not participated in active sports, although many said they were considered tomboys in their youth. In response to the question: "Are you a feminist?", 35 said yes, 5 no, and 11 "partly"; 36 did think their consciousness had been raised.

Concerning their Economic and Occupational Status, the majority had a gross income of between $10,000 and $20,000 and owned their own home. Of the sample, 11 were still working for pay, while 36 classified themselves as "retired" and 7 said they had no social security. Two-thirds of the respondents stated they had made financial provisions for their "old age"; for example, 39 had health insurance to supplement medicare. Only 8 identified themselves as "working class or blue-collar" lesbians.

Table II

Major Occupation During Work Life

Professional	34
Clerical	9
Industrial	0
Domestic	3
Farm	2
Other	7

(Some reported more than one category.)

The majority had been in the "helping professions." A small number, 7, had seen military service, and 10 had had some, usually temporary, experiences as a gym teacher or P.E. instructor.

The Physical/Mental Health profile of this group of women was as follows: 12 reported a physical handicap which they considered disabling, while 30 claimed to have had "major surgery." Of these, 8 had had hysterectomies and 2 had had mastectomies. Arthritis of some form was reported by 32 out of the 50. Weight-wise, 29 viewed themselves as too fat, whereas 18 felt they were "just right." Only 5 said they had had a "drinking problem," and the same number had had a "nervous breakdown." Physical or mental illness had institutionalized 4 respondents, 2 for depression, 1 for alcoholism, and 1 for surgery. One fifth reported having been in therapy sometime in the past. A large majority, 44, saw themselves as well-adjusted persons. While 9 were lonely, 20 preferred to live alone. Less than half were, or had ever been, members of a women's support group.

The survey indicated that these women were not, by and large, churchgoers: 12 indicated they attended religious services regularly, 30 claimed no religious affiliation whatever, and many of those who specified the "religious group" they belonged to did not mention one of the major religious or Christian denominations, but instead such organizations as Dignity, Gay Synagogue, and Christian Science. Only 4 reported any religious conflict because of their lifestyle. Another 7 admitted to being atheist, and 8 described themselves as "agnostic."

Table III

Self-Image

Excellent	16
Good	25
Fair	8
Poor	1

In response to questions about their Sexual Attitudes and Behavior, 11 confessed to having wanted to change their sex, but only when they were much younger; 32 expressed a "sympathetic" attitude toward transsexuals. Celibacy was an aspect of life for 34 of the respondents, and had been for from 3 months to 66 years. For 24 of these, their celibacy was not by choice. Two-thirds have been involved in cross-generation relationships, with age differences ranging from 20 to 53 years. Nearly all had masturbated, but only 10 had felt guilty about it. Few (15) had used a vibrator. Group sex was opposed by 28, and half the subjects believed in monogamy. None of the 9 who where presently in a committed relationship were or ever had been into role playing, or supported such behavior in others.

In response to the item which asked those who had had intimate relationships with both men and women to compare the two experiences, the expressions used most often to describe the woman-to-woman intimacy were: *more* emotional, caring, sharing, spiritual, gentle, sensitive, understanding, sympathetic, thoughtful, unselfish, desirable, with easier communication and less roleplaying. Women are less sexually demanding, less hurried, less mechanical, and more affectionate, intimate, and natural, with greater reciprocity on all levels. One commented that "marriage to a man is better than no relationship." Another indicated that "sexually there is not much difference."

In order of frequency of mention, "the most serious problems" which were confronting the participants at the time of the study were: health, finances, isolation, loneliness[13] and aging. Of the 50 who filled out the questionnaire, 6 claimed they had no serious problems. The replies to the next and final query, "How could a special social organization for older lesbians help?" reflected the concerns already expressed in the previous "problems" question, but in a rather different order of importance. Companionship was the most often listed, with contacts noted almost as frequently followed by health, recreation and relaxation, and other terms such as networking and parties, indicating the need for greater socialization.

DISCUSSION

Most people are aware that data can be interpreted to prove almost anything. This investigator would like to have been able to use the data collected here to support her long-held hypothesis that lesbians who have reached the age of 65 are survivors in more than just a physical sense, and are equipped to make a better adjustment to aging than their heterosexual female contemporaries.

Since the present research makes no attempt to compare the two groups and, as a study of hidden population, is not representative anyway, it may be obliquely instructive, in order to see what kind of an individual emerges, to look at a profile of the 65+ lesbian as constructed from the majority of answers to each item in the questionnaire.

Our subject is white, 5 ft., 6 in. tall, 68 years of age, weighs 140 lbs., was born in New York, and lives now in California. She has never married and is childless. She has no known gay relatives.

Her education and work experiences are above average and put her in the professional ranks. She holds a graduate degree and has retired from one of the helping professions in a government agency. Contrary to expectation, she has never attended, at any level, an all-girls' school or an educational institution that was church-affiliated. Nevertheless, she did meet the first woman she had a lesbian relationship within an educational setting. She is something of a free-thinker in that she does not subscribe to any formal religious belief nor attend any formal church services.

Our subject is not affluent, but neither is her annual income below the poverty line. But she is provident in that she has taken financial precautions for her old age. She lives in modest comfort. Her frugality has not allowed her to travel abroad widely, but she has visited both Canada and Mexico. She owns her own home where she involuntarily lives alone, drives a car less than 10 years old, and has a color TV on which she prefers to watch PBS programs. She is a non-smoker and drinks socially.

She does not participate in active sports. In spite of the fact she was considered a tomboy as a child, her preferred recreations are now more sedentary, in keeping with her maturity. She likes to garden and to read. She subscribes to *Ms* but has no favorite lesbian authors. However, her consciousness is raised and she considers herself a feminist. As a member of the Democratic Party who voted in the last election, she supports the ERA and would support a woman for president if one were nominated.

For entertainment outside the home, she prefers concerts. She never goes to women's bars and belongs to no social or professional lesbian groups, although she occasionally attends lesbian functions. She does not see herself as closeted and likes to spend her vacation with other lesbians.

Her self-image is good, and she has never been aware of being discriminated against for her lifestyle. She is not a separatist or a "radical" lesbian. She resents being called a "dyke" or "butch" and rejects S & M. While she expresses a sympathetic attitude toward transsexuals, she never wanted to be one. She thinks lesbians are less agist than heterosexual women but has not experienced age discrimination herself from either group.

Her appearance is somewhat more conservative than that of many younger lesbians. She sometimes wears dresses instead of slacks, wears lipstick as did most women of her generation, but does not use nail polish. Her hair is naturally gray and she does not have a permanent. She never had a face lift. She carries a purse but does not wear earrings or high heels, for she is not convinced that clothes reveal lifestyle. She wears pajamas to bed.

Although presently involuntarily celibate, unattached, and not in a committed union, she considers sex an integral part of a lesbian relationship. She has had, among other attachments, a cross-generational relationship involving an age difference of 20 years. She rejects group sex and believes in monogamy. She is not bisexual.

In spite of major surgery in the past and minor attacks of arthritis recently, her health is good. She has no physical handicap, no foot problems, and no false teeth. She wears glasses and her vision with them is good. She has never been in therapy or had a "nervous breakdown," and she considers herself a well-adjusted person. Although she does not prefer to live alone, she is not lonely and does not belong to any women's support group. She is apparently able to cope.

Thus described in profile, the 65+ lesbian seems to satisfy this researcher's hypothesis that these deviant women are, in their later maturity, survivors in more than just a physical sense and are equipped to make a better adjustment to aging than their heterosexual counterparts. Support for such a hypothesis will have to await additional investigation making the necessary comparison with an adequate control group of matching heterosexual women.

However, it must be said that this profile of a balanced, stable personality in no way discounts the disturbing problems of many lesbians over 65 not reached by this survey who may be living alone, either in an equally narrow-minded small-town enclave or in a culturally hostile community.

How many lesbians are in nursing homes or other health-care facilities where they must conceal their identity and live out their lives as strangers in a strange land? Or, subjected to poverty, how many must rely on unsympathetic counselors or advisors, or on insensitive social service providers in situations where they might be denied help if their affectional preference were known?

It is hoped that the dissemination of information, such as that collected in this survey, may help in educating the public to a greater awareness and acceptance of this section of the elderly population.

SUMMARY

This study attempts to gather information on a few of the million-plus lesbians over 65 estimated to be living in the United States as of 1980. It reviews some of the pioneer research efforts in the area of lesbian aging, describes how the data for the present survey was collected, and outlines the limitations of the research. Highlights of the results are set forth in some detail, while a profile of the "subject" is drawn from the majority of responses to each item in the questionnaire.

This composite profile presents a woman who might be anyone's grandmother, except that she never married or had any children. She is overweight, overeducated, liberal, and feminist, has enough income for moderate comfort, does not smoke, drinks only socially, likes to go to concerts, enjoys gardening and reading. She is not a joiner of either social or religious groups, and, not by preference, lives alone. She is healthy, both mentally and physically, and likes herself even though she knows she should lose weight.

Because of the "snowball" method of recruitment and self-selection of respondents, coupled with the inherent difficulties of reaching this hidden group at all, the present survey cannot be considered representative of any but a small and very select segment of the total population of lesbians over 65 in the United States.

APPENDIX A
Survey Cover Letter

San Francisco

March 1984

Dear Participant:

Women are reported to be the invisible half of the population. Of these the elderly are the more invisible and,

among the elderly, lesbians are the most invisible. Lesbians
come in all colors, religions, and size of pocketbooks. The
proposed study is intended to identify as many lesbians
over 65 as possible and, through an anonymous questionnaire, assess their needs.

This is the first step in establishing a network of communication to bring us out of our often self-imposed isolation
so that our needs can be met, our problems solved, and
our accomplishments recognized by an appropriate service
organization.

This organization, on the model of SAGE in New York
City, might provide the following services for those
incapacitated:

—sympathetic visiting at home, or in an institution;
—protective escort to hospitals for medical help, shop-
   ping, or necessary trips;
—telephone contact, especially for those house-bound or
   invalided;

and for others:

—social activities and a congenial meeting site for those
   lonely and depressed, where they can make new social
   contacts;
—bereavement support for those suffering the loss of a
   partner;
—information and referral for matters such as legal advice (about wills, e.g.), personal problems counseling,
   or direction to feminist medical clinics for consultation.

However, before any of this can be realized, lesbians over
65 must be located and descriptive data about them gathered.

The attached questionnaire has been developed by a
72-year-old lesbian, Monika Kehoe, PhD, a retired university professor, presently an Associate in the Center for
Research and Education in Sexuality at San Francisco
State University. It has been designed to collect information on the economic, physical, social, and psychological
condition of a sample group of lesbians, 65 years or older,
from all regions of continental United States.

Since almost nothing is known about the lives or outlook of lesbians in this age category, this survey hopes not only to collect data on their situation but also to learn something of their thinking in the area of sexual politics, their concerns and needs, and the kinds of social assistance that might help overcome the problems faced by this generally invisible and voiceless group of American senior citizens.

You have been selected to participate in this survey and we request your cooperation in answering the questions to the best of your ability. All information submitted will be treated with the strictest confidence. We request that no names be used and that the questionnaire be sent back by return mail, if possible, in the self-addressed, stamped envelope enclosed.

The data and information you provide will be used in developing an extended report which we hope will give us all a better understanding of the lives and outlook of senior lesbians in America. If you live in the San Francisco Bay Area and are willing to be interviewed, please send me your name, address, and phone number separately.

All questionnaires are completely anonymous, and participants in the study must freely consent to answering the questionnaire. There is no obligation to participate and no pecuniary reward.

Thank you for joining us in this project.

Monika Kehoe

NOTES

1. The program of the annual Conference of the Gerontological Society of America, held in San Francisco in November of 1983, gave no recognition to the existence of aging lesbians or gay men.

2. For a criticism of feminist insensitivity to the issue of sexual identity in classic feminist works, see Adrienne Rich's essay, "Compulsory heterosexuality and lesbian experience" in *The signs reader: Women, gender and scholarship.* (eds. E. and E. K. Abel, University of Chicago Press, 1983.) pp. 139–168.

3. *The Journal of Homosexuality*, recognized as the leading academic periodical in the field, has not had an article dealing with lesbianism and the old-old. One entitled "Growing older female: Heterosexuality and homosexuality," by M. Laner, in the Spring 1979 issue, included no lesbians in their "later maturity" (63 to 80 years of age).

4. Berger, R. (1982). *Gay and gray.* Urbana, IL: University of Illinois Press.

5. Starr, B., & Weiner, M. (1981–1982). *The Starr-Weiner Report on Sex and Sexuality in the Mature Years*. New York: Stein & Day.

6. For an overall review of the literature on lesbianism, see Chapter II of the Chris Almvig study.

7. The findings were first made public at the May 1983 meeting of the Anthropological Research Group in Sacramento, CA, and at the June 1983 conference of the National Association of Lesbian and Gay Gerontologists, held at San Francisco State University.

8. Finally, perhaps another distinctive feature that might be mentioned is that the principal investigator is a 77-year-old life-long lesbian who began to work on this project in 1980 when she was associated with Americas Behavioral Research Corporation, a federally-funded organization in San Francisco which lost its grant at the advent of the Reagan administration. In April of 1982 the project was transferred to the Center for Research and Education in Sexuality (CERES) located within the Psychology Department of San Francisco State University. Dr. Kehoe was assisted there by Sheryl Goldberg, MSW, who reported on the results of the research at the November 1983 meeting of the Gay Academic Union in San Diego, CA. Acknowledgement must also be given for the important contribution of Brenda Spinner, PhD, who did the statistical work and prepared the tables which accompany this article. Besides this, her overall advice as a psychologist specializing in Gerontology was invaluable.

9. S. F. Morin, in his 1977 article "Heterosexual bias in psychological research on lesbianism and male homosexuality" (*American Psychologist, 32*, 629–637), stated that there is no such thing as a representative sample of a hidden population.

10. Courtesy of the Associated Students Women's Center of San Francisco State University.

11. A copy of the letter appears in Appendix A.

12. The postage cost was a total of 74 cents for each mailing. This was covered by a grant from Cimenatherapy Inc. of San Francisco, the only financial support received for the entire project.

13. In view of the recent focus on pet therapy for the elderly, it is regrettable that this question was not included.

A Note on May Sarton

Margaret Cruikshank, PhD

San Francisco City College

Although lesbian writers and writing have been discussed from a feminist perspective for at least 15 years, defining these terms remains a perplexing task.[1]

In an article I wrote in 1980 on autobiographical works by lesbians, I excluded May Sarton because, in her memoirs and journals, she did not seem to regard her lesbianism as a central fact of her life. The writers I was describing, on the other hand, were self-consciously, even triumphantly, lesbian. In Sarton's writings, relationships between lesbians were only a peripheral subject, whereas they were main themes in works such as Kate Millett's *Flying* and Mary Meigs' *Lily Briscoe: A self portrait*. I speculated that May Sarton would not call herself a "lesbian writer" because she would consider the label limiting.

Three years later, after meeting Sarton for an interview, I began to question my exclusion of her from the article on autobiographical writing.[2] She did not fit my stereotype of the semi-closeted older woman, for she was very knowledgeable about lesbian and gay politics and clearly moved in gay social circles. She talked of a lesbian writer new to me, Sylvia Townsend Warner, and nothing in Sarton's poetry or fiction would have led me to expect her witty remarks about clothing and butch-femme styles.

Obviously, a writer's persona should not be confused with her real life identity. Nevertheless, the experience of talking to May Sarton helped me understand that excluding her work from my article was a political rather than a

---

Dr. Cruikshank teaches gay and lesbian literature at the City College of San Francisco, and has edited three anthologies: *The Lesbian Path* (1980), *Lesbian Studies* (1982), and *New Lesbian Writing* (1984). Reprint requests may be sent to the author, Department of English, City College of San Francisco, 50 Phelan Avenue, San Francisco, CA 94112.

153

literary choice, one that revealed my inability to place her *inside* the lesbian feminist movement. I wanted her writing to celebrate lesbianism, not merely allude to it. This unstated criterion required that the writer have a particular temperament and emotional history, that she be a certain kind of lesbian. If, however, a lesbian writer is more broadly defined as a woman whose creative work sheds light on lesbian lives past and present, then Sarton is easily included. If the critic insists on seeing citizenship papers before admitting writers to Lesbian Nation, she may miss not only women of Sarton's generation, but also others whose independence keeps them from political alignments.

In a recent interview in the *Paris Review,* May Sarton said, "The militant lesbians want me to be a militant and I'm just not" (No. 89, Fall 1983, p. 86). Here she suggests a conflict of interest between the movement's need for heroes, outspoken and preferably famous, and the writer's need to steer her own course. But by allowing her lesbianism to be more visible in recent years, for example in the film *A World of Light* and in the *Paris Review* interview, Sarton has contributed to the public discussion of homosexuality. As long as the subject remains controversial, the writer who treats it will be seen as a spokesperson, whether or not that role is congenial. Often it is onerous; Jane Rule has said that "writers are by nature solitary, willful and perverse and have no business leading anybody anywhere."[3]

Lesbian/gay politics and literature are inextricably joined. Without the women's movement and the gay rights movement, phrases such as "lesbian literature" and "gay studies" would be inconceivable. Nevertheless, the tension between literature and politics should at least be acknowledged, if we are to avoid, in Orwell's phrase, the "worst follies of orthodoxy." Admiring May Sarton's bravery for publishing a novel with a lesbian protagonist in the mid-1960s, *Mrs. Stevens Hears the Mermaids Singing,* lesbian feminist readers perhaps wanted Sarton to be a public figure, a sage in the manner of Audre Lorde or Adrienne Rich. But solitude and independence have not only been natural choices for Sarton; they seem pre-conditions for her art.

NOTES

1. Virginia Woolf exemplifies the problem of deciding who is a lesbian writer. Her affair with Vita Sackville-West is well known, and other women fell in love with Woolf as well, including the redoubtable Ethel Smyth. In her *Letters*, however, the word "sapphist" appears as a description for other women only, not for herself, and she uses it in a faintly derisive way. On the other hand, Woolf wrote to her sister, Vanessa Bell, "You will never succumb to the charms of any of your sex—What an arid garden the world must be for you." (May 22, 1927, *Letters*, Vol. III, 381). But this lovely declaration probably has more to do with sibling rivalry than with self-definition: Having discovered an experience, a slightly scandalous one unknown to her sister, Woolf cannot resist boasting.

2. The article is "Notes on Recent Lesbian Autobiographical Writing," *Journal of Homosexuality* (1982), *8* (1), 19–26. The interview is "May Sarton: A Woman and a Poet Apart," *The Advocate* (1983, August 18), pp. 41–43.

3. Geoff Mains, "Jane Rule: Music from Diverse Instruments," (interview), *The Advocate* (1984, February 7), p. 45.

A Portrait of the Older Lesbian

Monika Kehoe, PhD
San Francisco State University

Feminist writers tell us that women are invisible and have been for as long as history has been recorded. Except for the performance of a few queens or other national leaders such as Margaret Thatcher, who are generally presented as having been really "just like men," the contributions of women in every field have been ignored. Women have no place in the "The Ascent of Man," as you will have seen if you watched that overrated, masculinist television "special" a few years ago. Not until the advent of Women's Studies has the academic curriculum provided us with any but the most meager information on women's achievement.

But even among the invisible half of the population, there are some who are more invisible than others: the aged. A youth-oriented culture like ours in the West doesn't want to be reminded about aging. Even though women outnumber men by almost two to one in the over-60 age group, gerontology and geriatrics focus on the male. There are very few studies, and even fewer college courses, devoted exclusively to the aging process and related problems of the female. The older woman appears under the all-inclusive label of "the elderly."[1]

Yet there is a category of older women who make up a still more hidden subculture: the aging lesbian. This group has been studied even less. And no wonder. Anyone over 60 in 1985 grew up in an era when homosexuality was unmentionable, unthinkable, a sin, a crime, a disease, and for the great majority of the population, unheard of. Even

---

Correspondence should be addressed to Dr. Kehoe, 87 Banks Street, San Francisco, CA 94110.

[1]How much of this invisibility is a result of the masculine structure of the English language is yet to be fully determined. (See Nilsen, A. P., Bosmajian, H., Gershuny, H. L., & Stanley, J. P., *Sexism and language*, National Council Teachers of English, Urbana, IL 1977.)

Simone de Beauvoir in her monumental work, *The Coming of Age* (1970), which the *New York Times Book Review* described as the confrontation of "a subject of universal private anguish and universal public silence," deals only incidentally with women throughout the 864 pages of her text and exclusively with men in her brief reference to homosexuality, (pp. 12–14).[2]

As a result, the lesbian over 60 is likely to be a very private person, difficult to flush out and, even when found, reticent about her past as well as her present. She has little of the compulsion of later generations of homosexual women who are eager to make a political statement about their lifestyle. After all, she has spent her "three-score" keeping a low profile, not necessarily ashamed of her same-gender emotional-erotic identification but concerned rather about holding her job in a much less permissive era. And remember, she lived through the McCarthy period.[3]

When her job was an academic one, she was under more severe scrutiny than ever, especially if she was teaching in an all-women's college, either secular or church-affiliated. In the latter, the usually female administration, who were not supposed to know about such things but could probably have written their own version of "The Children's Hour," tended to be particularly wary of student-teacher crushes. Seldom was anything on this subject mentioned in these "female seminaries," except perhaps for a conversational reminder of the college policy that forbade single "lay" faculty from entertaining students individually at home. As a result, the homosexual academic woman, who was more likely to be found in a women's college than anywhere else for obvious reasons of preferential employment (there were no affirmative action programs then), she had to be cautious in the extreme.

Career was most always of primary concern for her. If she was not a bisexual, or a late (post-divorce or post-husband's demise) convert to the homosexual life, she had no

<hr>

[2]Translated by Patrick O'Brien, New York: Putman, 1972.
[3]For a review of a study of *working* lesbians in the early decades of the century, see: Bullough & Bullough, Lesbianism in the 1920's and 1930's: A Newfound Study, *Signs, 2*(4), 895–904.

one to support her financially and oftentimes was ostra-
cized by her family, and was thus left with no place to
turn. She had to be self-sufficient, had to keep her job.
There were no food stamps or welfare checks for such
women, with or without dependents. As professional
workers they had no Social Security to look forward to
either.

But a 60-year-old-plus life-long lesbian is bound to be a
survivor. Consider how many there must be out there,
some living alone having lost their partners, others in
couples cherishing each other in their "golden years," as
the senior-citizens brochures like to call it; few of them
suffering the traumas of widowhood that so many heterosexual women undergo. Trained in independence, often
without family support in their youth, these lesbians have
learned to make their own way, to buck the system, to
make the necessary compromises with society, out of necessity, to plan for retirement.

The self-image of these women is good and does not
conform to the regular assessment: The older woman is
what she looks like, whereas the older man is what he
does. Since they have usually escaped the beauty-shop pro-
gramming and the post-menstrual syndrome fear of their
heterosexual counterparts who view the advent of middle
age with trepidation and anxiety, they are relieved of most
of the pressures that afflict the aging women in "normal"
society. Many of those who remained single may have retained their youth in a more subtle way. Without having
been forced to assume the customary roles of wife, mother,
and grandmother, they escaped the expectations that society places on other more culturally compliant and domesticated women as they move from one stage in life to the
next. As we see from the recent survey (Kehoe, this issue),
those lesbians with advanced degrees who have been in
academe or other professions have remained single; as a
result, their lives have not been marked by, nor have their
attitudes been sculptured by, the rites of passage that dramatize family events. They are less likely to perceive that
life is over for them, or to give up and "let themselves go,"
as they leave mid-life behind them.

Gynophiles[4] in academe and the other professional fields
who are without family ties have had wider options and
more mobility in their working lives. Without maternal re-
sponsibilities, they have had more time to advance their
careers, to pursue the activities (including sports) of their
youth into old age, and to continue to associate with the
young and to think young. Without the strictures and op-
pressions of the prevalent patriarchal family life, they
could develop a consciousness beyond the confines of conventional wisdom. Their advanced education, more unusual for women then, gave them the opportunity for
greater insight and a more critical evaluation of traditional
behavior patterns. They were liberated long before "wom-
en's liberation" became a movement.

Besides being better adjusted to aging, the gynophile
who has retired from university teaching or one of the
other professions is more often, by choice, a solitary and
reserved person. There were no gay networks in her day—
no Dignity, no Wishing Well, no League, and no place set
aside as "womanspace." There was no "women's building"
sponsoring feminist activities and no feminist bookstores
for the circulation of radical or deviant revolutionary ideas,
much less lesbian literature. There was no gay "community" as such, even in the largest metropolitan areas, and
few if any women's bars existed. Where they did exist, they
were in a tough section of the city and, in spite of the
"protection" demanded of their management, which was
usually male, the bars were frequently raided by the vice
squads. Their clientele was mainly what would now be considered the leather-jacket set. Such places were not likely
to attract those women who valued their jobs, particularly
if they were in higher education. And, in the depression
era of the thirties, except for the Paris salons of a Gertie
Stein or a Natalie Barney, private parties for gay women
were much less common than today.

Nevertheless, the retired academic gynophile who is

---

[4]I've coined this word to express and encompass those extra dimensions of
the woman-to-woman relationship which the word *lesbian* somehow fails to
include—at least for gay women of the pre-World War II period, as well as for
all those for whom intellectual and emotional compatibility is paramount and
for whom genitality is not crucial. (See the article by Judith Schwartz entitled
Questionnaire on Issues in Lesbian History, in *Frontiers*, Fall 1979, pp. 4–5).

alone at sixty or beyond is less likely to be lonely. She has wider solitary, scholarly interests. Although she may miss a lost partner with whom she spent many years, she is often able to "live alone and like it" much more comfortably than her heterosexual, widowed contemporary. She has not been the dependent half of a couple; she can continue to manage her own affairs. Or, in the framework of the new mores, she can seek out another relationship. She is not so likely to be homebound or remain isolated in suburbia. She is not so intimidated to go out alone. Solitude gives her the chance to read all the books she has never been able to enjoy because of her demanding work schedule and her need to keep up with her professional field. At long last, she has time to write. These are precious privileges circumscribed by days that are too short.

But not all older lesbians (to return to the more conventional term) prefer to live alone. Where are they to meet other "mature" women with their lifestyle? Does their greater resiliency make it easier for them to find partners than for older women in the heterosexual population? Probably it is since death takes such a heavy toll of men in the over-60 age group. Can two (or more) aging dykes share the same kitchen? Can they live communally in ways that will be a model for their heterosexual counterparts? Or must each one maintain her individual refrigerator, stove, bathroom? Surely, even without models of their own to follow, lesbians should have escaped, or at least resisted, the traditional thinking that women of the same generation cannot share living space happily for an extended period of time. Their life experience has been different; sharing a home should be easier for them. And it is clearly healthier not to live alone, especially as one grows older. The aging lesbian couple, still so hidden, can be a role model, caring for each other in a society in which women over 60 increasingly outnumber men in the same age group.

BOOK REVIEWS

SCOTCH VERDICT. L. Faderman. *New York: Quill, 1983.*

Lillian Faderman's book *Scotch Verdict* illuminates a critical moment in lesbian history. Although the incident the book describes took place nearly 200 years ago, its mysteries continue to haunt our lives in the 1980s.

Scotch Verdict tells the story of the 19th century Scottish case involving two school-mistresses accused of lesbianism by one of their pupils. Marianne Woods and Jane Pirie had opened a boarding school in Edinburgh in 1809 in the hopes of freeing themselves from lives as governesses. They would be independent women, they conjectured, with control over their own lives. Woods and Pirie had been friends for several years, and Faderman defines their friendship as a "romantic" one, a type of bond between women that was accepted, in fact encouraged, by 19th century Scottish culture. What could be more perfect, then, than a partnership that would let these two friends live their lives together and share their aspirations?

By Christmas of that year, they had accepted Jane Cumming as one of their pupils. Jane was the granddaughter of the socially prominent and politically powerful Dame Helen Cumming Gordon. She was also half East Indian, the illegitimate daughter of George Cumming's liaison with a 15-year-old Indian woman he met during his tour of the Asian subcontinent. Woods and Pirie debated over the wisdom of admitting her as a pupil. She was, as one of the judges would remark later, "lacking in the advantages of a European complexion." But because of the social position of Dame Cumming Gordon, who could send other notable young scholars their way, they accepted Jane Cumming into their school. That decision sealed their fate.

One weekend, Jane Cumming went home and told her grandmother that Woods and Pirie were lovers. She said she had seen them make love together on several occasions and she provided graphic details and tantalizing bits of conversations to back up her statements. Within 24 hours, all the students had been withdrawn from Woods's and Pirie's school. In a gallant effort to save their reputations, the teachers sued Dame Cumming Gordon for libel. More than 10 years later, when the case was finally settled, Woods and Pirie received about 1,000 pounds in damages; the original suit had demanded 10,000. Their friendship had been destroyed and the popular conception of female sexuality seriously challenged.

As Faderman has pointed out, the public in 19th century Scotland had no trouble believing in homosexuality—just in *female* homosexuality. By 1811, there had been several cases of males found guilty of sodomy and cases involving female transvestites. But those issues were different from lesbianism, which was commonly thought to be a physical as well as an emotional impossibility. Freud had yet to indoctrinate the popular mind with the idea that lesbianism was the result of a repressed libido. In fact, women were thought to have "no sexuality to repress." They were passionless vessels, beings who guarded the public (i.e., male) morality. The thought of a passionate sexual relationship between two women not only challenged the accepted understanding of female nature, but also threatened to topple the entire groundwork upon which 19th century sexual morality was built.

Faderman's book is a marvelous interdisciplinary experiment. It's part history: She rigorously researched the court transcripts, and her understanding of the cultural message embodied in the court's decision has put into perspective a pivotal moment in 19th century history. At the same time, she endows the book with certain aspects of fiction: A first-person "partly autobiographical" narrator discusses the case with the reader as she researches it. She speculates from a 20th-century lesbian perspective what is a complicated and confusing issue.

The questions surrounding the case are still not re-solved. Were Pirie and Woods really lovers? Or did Jane Cumming fabricate the story based on sexual information she learned in India? If Jane was lying, what was her motive? If Pirie and Woods were lovers, why were they so careless? And what did the embarrassment of a public trial do to all their lives? Little is known outside of the details provided by the public transcript. Faderman manages to trace Woods to London where she found a teaching job. Pirie remained in Edinburgh where she eked out a meager existence until the case was settled. Jane Cumming's trail was lost in her early 20's. How did these three protagonists in this important case live out the rest of their lives? How did they die? Faderman provides some fascinating theories from which the readers can draw their own conclusions.

And what of the judges, the seven men who handed down the "Scotch verdict." Faderman points out the important elements of race, sex, and class that were involved in their decision. If they decided that the teachers were lesbians, they admitted that women were sexual beings and threw suspicion on the whole institution of "romantic friendship." If they found Dame Cumming Gordon guilty of libel, they ruled against a member of their own class and social circle. If they believed Jane Cumming's story, they doubted the word of two pious Scottish women. But on the other hand, if they doubted the girl, they took the word of the middle class over the granddaughter of an aristocrat. Small wonder, then, that their first decision was in favor of Cumming Gordon by a single vote and the second in favor of the teachers by the same margin. No matter what the judges decided, they had to re-evaluate some element of their basic understanding of how the world worked and how women fit into it.

Betsy Swart

MADAME AURORA. S. Aldridge. *Tallahassee, FL: Naiad Press, 1983.*

Madame Aurora is a thoroughly engaging historical novel about an older lesbian couple and two younger women who fall in love. Set in the years following the Civil War, the story focuses on the economic struggle of a scholar, Elizabeth, and her life-partner, Hannah, who assumes the identity of a psychic, Madame Aurora, to earn money. Madame Aurora is probably the only character in lesbian fiction who makes a killing on the stock market. She does so with the profits from her spiritual business. She seems as much a therapist as a psychic. Through flashbacks we learn of the earlier life of Elizabeth and Hannah. Elizabeth's scholarship has been ignored by men, but is highly valued by young Nell Purcell, a worker at the Library of Congress, who meets Elizabeth there. Nell's friend is the niece of a wealthy woman who depends on Madame Aurora for advice and support. A rather Dickensian sub-plot involves the husband of Madame Aurora's patron. Aldridge's fluent, graceful prose and her storytelling skills are impressive. In addition, *Madame Aurora* sheds light on 19th-century lesbian history by showing how limited were the wage-earning possibilities for single women, who had to be extremely resourceful if they were to lead independent lives.

Margaret Cruikshank, PhD

THE INVISIBLE MINORITY: AGING AND LESBIANISM. C. Almvig. *New York: Utica College of Syracuse University, 1982.*

Research exclusively on the life experiences of older lesbians is extremely limited. In her descriptive study, *The Invisible Minority: Aging and Lesbianism,* Chris Almvig fulfills her intention of "shedding light on this neglected group of women."

Almvig is a pioneer in the field of lesbian and gay aging. Not only has she published the first informative account of older lesbians, but she was also the co-founder of Senior Action in Gay Environment (S.A.G.E.) in New York City, the first social service agency for older lesbians and gays in the country. In her continuing efforts to improve the life satisfaction of this group, Almvig is in the process of developing a retirement community for them in the New York metropolitan area.

The Invisible Minority investigates the lives of a national sample of 74 lesbians over 50. Three thousand copies of the 44-item questionnaire, which included additional topics for comment, were distributed by placing ads in lesbian publications and through mailings to lesbian and gay groups nationwide, as well as through personal contacts. In addition to demographic data, her inquiry explores respondents' self-perception of mental health, thoughts about aging and agism, family relationships and support systems, preparations for the future, values in relationships, and connections to the gay and non-gay communities. This sample group of lesbians was weighted towards white, well-educated, employed women between the ages of 50 and 60 who lived in urban settings on the West Coast and in the Northeast. Almost half the respondents had been married sometime in their lives. In relation to the high level of academic achievement of the respondents, Almvig indicates that, "it has been suggested that perhaps when women realize and come to grips with the fact that they are lesbians and are willing to seek out a lifestyle according to that fact, they are also going to need to develop a plan for becoming self-sufficient. On the other hand, these respondents may be more responsive to a research survey."

The majority of subjects indicated that they were mentally healthy, that their lesbianism had been a "source of great joy and satisfaction," and that they felt positive about their aging. When questioned about fears relating to aging, many reported apprehension around the loss of physical or mental capabilities and around financial difficulties. Concerning relationships, half were interested in partners/lovers of the same age. Many in this group visited "safe places such as lesbian organizations, and friendship networks" to meet socially. Almost all said they received emotional support from other lesbians. About 75 percent had been with women for over 20 years, women Almvig referred to as "life-long" lesbians. Of these women, 10 percent had been in relationships with women lasting from 20 to 30 years. The remaining "late-blooming" lesbians had come out in their middle to later years.

The majority of respondents prepared for old age by keeping intellectually stimulated, financially solvent, and physically fit (including a healthy diet and exercise). The "additional comments" section of the questionnaire explored individual lesbian histories. By asking them for in-depth reports, Almvig collected information that would otherwise be available only by personal interviews. She concludes in her summary that, "being still secret may be the biggest determining factor concerning how an older lesbian will be affected by her aging."

The implications of this study include an obligation for members of the lesbian community to organize and take action on behalf of the group's interests. "Researchers can provide the hard data needed to help justify social and legal change." The findings can provide assessment and evaluation of the group and its needs in order to help facilitate development and expansion of lesbian and gay senior service organizations such as S.A.G.E. in New York anb G.L.O.E. (Gay and Lesbian Outreach to Elders) in San Francisco.

Almvig's investigation of this "invisible minority" is informative and comprehensive. She expands the data presented by adding information regarding her personal experiences and work with older lesbians. Her inclusion of conceptual definitions, an extensive literature review, and bibliography are extremely valuable in interpreting the overall findings of her study. In her statistical presentation of these, Almvig appropriately incorporates the comments of her respondents. When addressing information specific to aging policies and practice, she draws from documents such as reports from the Federal Council on Aging.

In her introduction, the researcher speaks to what she considers the deficiencies of the study. They include: (1) the absence of comparisons between heterosexual women or gay men; (2) the omissions of questions pertaining to alcohol use or abuse; (3) the lack of personal interviews; and (4) the limitations of the sample to white, well-educated respondents of relatively high socio-economic status. This study might have been additionally strengthened by including: (1) more investigation into the family relationships of the respondents, specifically those who had children and, if no children, feelings about this; and (2) inclusion of more lesbians over the age of 60. A majority (65%) of the respondents were between the ages of 50 and 60; only 6 were over 60. Additional efforts need to be made to identify and investigate the "older" lesbian and the "old-old" lesbian, those 60 to 75 and those 75 plus, respectively.

Almvig's account of the lives of 74 lesbians over 50 provides those interested in social gerontological issues with a substantive base of knowledge from which to develop an awareness of older lesbians; such an awareness would in turn facilitate efforts to provide services for this group. Perhaps even more importantly, this study offers lesbians of all ages information which may help with the confrontation, understanding, and appreciation of our own aging processes. Since models for aging and successful aging are difficult to find in the lesbian community, such information is critical.

Sheryl Goldberg, MSW

NEW LESBIAN WRITING. M. Cruikshank (Ed.). *San Francisco: Grey Fox Press, 200 pages, 1984.*

New Lesbian Writing, edited by Margaret Cruikshank, is one of the highlights of recent feminist pulishing. Bringing together the work of 35 women, each with a voice distinctly her own, Cruikshank has done an outstanding job of selecting and arranging material in this eclectic collection. The works range stylistically from the experimental, Linda-Jean Brown's "jazz dancin wif mama" and Beth Brant's dream-like narrative "A Simple Act," to the conventional, an essay by Jane Rule responding to her critics, and auto-biographical excerpts by Canadian poet Elsa Gidlow. Also included are works in which some traditional forms are put to new uses. Suniti Namjoshi entertains and instructs with a lesbian sensibility in her "Feminist Fables," while love poem by M. S. Andrews structurally imitates the form of a fugue.

The contributors in this collection are of diverse cultural backgrounds, including American Indian, Black, Chinese-American, and Jewish. Women from India, Jamaica, Australia, Canada, and the United States, lesbians over 65, lesbian mothers, working-class lesbians, and lesbian academicians are all represented here. The collection is unified not only by the lesbianism of its contributors but also by their skill as writers.

The poetry selection which begins the book sets a tone of playful and affirmative self-assertion which is echoed throughout. Martha Courtot reflects in her poem "Lesbian Bears":

> I have seen lesbian plums which cling to each other
> in the tightest of monogamous love
> and I have watched lesbian pumpkins
> declare the whole patch their playground
> profligate & dusky
> their voices arouse something in us
> which is laughing
>
> ah, everything is lesbian which loves itself
> I am lesbian when I really look in the mirror
> the world is lesbian in the morning & the evening
> only in mid-afternoon does it try to pretend
> otherwise . . .
>
> admit it   you too   would like to   love yourself. . . .

Other poems explore the themes of identity, partnership, transition, family, and community. Many, like Audrey Ewart's "Beneath My Hands," celebrate sensuality:

> How will you be
> beneath my hands

will you be soft and firm
full and round
will you tremble
as I range over your hills
and slide into your furrows
will you open
bud by bud
or will you burst
into full flower
will your voice rise high
run deep
or purr . . .

The poetry/prose division of the book is visually effective but slightly misleading, since many of the "prose" pieces, like Paula Gunn Allen's "In the Shadows Singing She Remembered," are in essence lyrical. Separating the poetry and prose sections is a third section which includes photographs of the contributors.

A fascinating piece by Barbara Deming recalls her travels in Greece in the 1950s from a perspective 20 years later. In longer autobiographical selections, Elsa Gidlow, Monika Kehoe, and Mary Meigs reflect on their recognition of their own lesbianism and its reception by others. These selections are moving evidence of an aspect of lesbian history all too often unacknowledged: There were lesbians leading courageous, affirmative, and uncompromising lives long before the women's movement of the 1970s.

Two short pieces, a story by Ethel Florence Lindsay Richardson never before published in the United States, and a new translation of Renee Vivien's "Prince Charming," break the continuity of the collection and seem to have been included more to increase the breadth of the anthology than for their own intrinsic merits.

Lesbian writers publishing today have the historically unprecedented opportunity to reach an audience to whom their lesbianism does not need to be explained or defended. Unlike much of the lesbian writing of the 1970s, which tended to focus didactically on lesbianism in its struggle to end the social invisibility of lesbians, the selections in *New Lesbian Writing* are not devoted primarily to analyzing the experience of being a lesbian. Instead, they tend to take that experience for granted and leave the task of analysis largely in the hands of the reader. Precisely because it represents the work of a diverse group, this anthology succeeds in challenging the reader without resorting to polemics.

Cruikshank was a pioneer of the lesbian-feminist anthological tradition. Her first collection, *The Lesbian Path*, was one of the earliest collections of autobiographical writings by lesbians. Her subsequent *Lesbian Studies* was a landmark work establishing the credibility of lesbian studies in an academic context and making lesbian issues visible and virtually impossible to ignore in women's studies curricula. Reflecting Cruikshank's academic training, *New Lesbian Writing* features an outstanding bibliography of lesbian literature, criticism, and periodicals, and includes introductory notes on recent developments in lesbian-feminist publishing.

I must take exception to one point in the introduction. Cruikshank states, "Those who raise questions of standards and excellence, however, sail into dangerous waters where accusations of patriarchal elitism await them. Since the identity of writer empowers women, it is difficult to challenge anyone's claim to that identity." While traditional standards of excellence have often reflected patriarchal (racist, sexist, classist, agist) biases and while I readily acknowledge the need to challenge and re-define such standards, I cannot bring myself to believe that judgements to quality are entirely irrelevant or subjective, or that they should be rejected entirely. The very excellence of the writing in this anthology, from the point of view of the writer's craft, leads me to question whether Cruikshank herself completely appreciates the literary merits of her contributors. I wish she had taken more pains to express her point clearly, and that she had placed it elsewhere. Coming as it does at the end of an otherwise well-executed introduction, her remark seems to be offered almost as a disclaimer. While such a statement would have been relevant in *The Lesbian Path*, it is patently inappropriate here, where most of the contributors are self-identified writers.

Originally conceived as a text for lesbian and gay studies

and women's studies, *New Lesbian Writing* clearly transcends its original intent. The quality of the writing will appeal to a wide audience. In light of the spirit of self-acceptance, insight, humor, and joyfulness its contributors inspire, this collection can be a lasting source of enjoyment.

Barbara Ustanko

Index